PODCASTING

How to Start a Podcast and Create
a Profitable Podcasting Business

AMANDA MAYO

Published by *Monkey Publishing*

Author: *Amanda Mayo*

Edited by *Lily Marlene Booth*

Cover Design by *Diogo Lando*

ISBN: 9781677650200

ASIN: B082KZYNBB

1st Edition, published in 2019

© 2019 by Monkey Publishing

Lerchenstrasse 111

22767 Hamburg

Germany

MONKEY PUBLISHING

OUR HAND-PICKED
BOOK SELECTION FOR YOU.

LEARN
SOMETHING NEW
EVERYDAY.

Table of Content

Introduction

Podcasts are a hugely popular way to consume audio, information, stories, and find inspiration. Communities are built around the niches podcasts serve and more and more news outlets are turning to podcasting to deliver the day's events in an easy to listen to short audio package. The future is here and it is only going to get bigger and better.

Podcasts are democratic in nature. They are not regulated by the government and have international reach thanks to the internet. They are also largely free to listen to. In many ways podcasting is like the Wild West of media and we're still at the forefront watching it develop. There is or can be a podcast for anything.

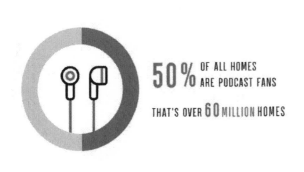

50% OF ALL HOMES ARE PODCAST FANS

THAT'S OVER 60 MILLION HOMES

In 2019 51% of the U.S. population listened to podcasts regularly with 80% of that number listening to full episodes. Further, an average of 7 shows are listened to each week. To translate percentages for you 60 million U.S. households[1] listen to podcasts. Those

[1] Statistics from https://www.podcastinsights.com/podcast-statistics/

numbers steadily, and sometimes dramatically, increase each year.

The State of Podcasting

% of respondents in selected countries who listened to any podcast in the past month

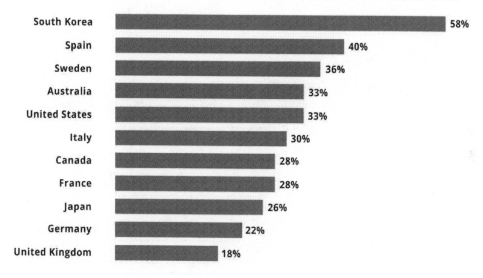

South Korea	58%
Spain	40%
Sweden	36%
Australia	33%
United States	33%
Italy	30%
Canada	28%
France	28%
Japan	26%
Germany	22%
United Kingdom	18%

You have things to say, you have expertise in something no one else does because you are you. Podcasting is how you can connect to the world. Be bold, be brave, be creative, find your niche and with it your audience. Are you ready to brave the frontier of media by sharing your voice with the world? Here's how...

This book is a comprehensive guide to get you well on your way to hosting a successful podcast. Everything you need to know to get from square one to a finished podcast is in this book. Planning is key to execution with a project as big as a podcast, but it doesn't have to be complicated. The steps to getting your podcast off the ground are: conceptualizing, storyboarding, landing on a podcast format/theme, bringing your content to life effectively, recording, editing, launching, marketing, and monetizing.

The most successful podcasts are niche and have a clear vision paired with a quality delivery. I'll go in depth on how to conceptualize your show using storyboarding as a guide. Format options will help you decide on what makes the most sense for your content. The benefits of co-hosting and how to choose a valuable partner for your podcast is covered. An in-depth tutorial on how to interview someone will set you up for success and get you great tape.

I'll help you navigate identifying and speaking to your audience through each step to ensure you are growing and maintaining your listeners. Detailed recommendations on the best equipment for the thrifty as well as those who have a larger budget are included, as well as tips for getting the best possible recording no matter where you are.

Lastly, I'll give you the ins and outs of how to launch your podcast successfully. Unfortunately, making the thing and putting it out into the world won't result in an immediate following. You need to know how to build your community ahead of time and how to best get the word out about your awesome podcast. Not only will I talk about launch strategy, but also marketing and monetization.

If you take everything in this guide to heart, you'll be able to start and maintain the podcast of your dreams. My advice is always to listen and soak up the information in this book. It comes from over a decade's worth of first-hand experience in radio and podcasting. Listen to yourself to keep improving. Listen to your audience and give them what they want while staying true to yourself. Listen to the world around you – anything can change at the drop of a hat, use that to your advantage to always be adjusting. Listen to your gut. Be realistic about your time and limitations. Whether you're creating something that will change the world or just make it a little bit more tolerable to live in, your podcast is important. Use the information provided here to make it the best it can be. You're setting yourself up for success already, so let's get started!

1. The Conceptual Nuts and Bolts of Making a Podcast

The origins of the podcast come from broadcast radio. The special programs you would hear on a radio station that fill about an hour of time, such as *"This American Life,"* or *"Freakonomics."* These programs range from game show style, *"Wait, Wait, Don't Tell Me"* to storytelling, *"The Moth"* to investigative journalism specific to the area where you are listening. Typically, the design of a radio program includes a dedicated topic that the host can cover in depth. Either through investigative journalism, storytelling, interviewing experts to offer differing perspectives, or a combination of these options. This format is similar to writing a paper, there is an established thesis supported by facts and perspectives, and then a conclusion provided by the writer.

Podcasting began in 2004 thanks to MTV video jockey Adam Curry and software developer Dave Winer. They developed a program, affectionately named iPodder, that could automatically download radio programs to an iPod. As it stands today (2020), podcasting is not regulated by the government. This means a podcaster does not need to purchase a broadcast license to exist. This also means podcasts do not need to adhere to the Federal Communication Commission's (FCC) guidelines.

Which we will talk about more in chapter 7: *if your podcast will be played on air of a radio station with a broadcasting license.*

The wonderful thing about this unregulated model is that you can develop the format that suits you. If you want your podcast to sound like a 48-minute radio show similar to, *"This American Life"* or *"Wait, Wait, Don't Tell Me"* you can. If you want to break the mold with a twelve-minute podcast interviewing interesting people on the street, or tackle daily hard-hitting political content in 30-minutes you have that option. There is a plethora of podcasts available in the world, so it is important to understand what you want to bring to the market.

Understanding Why you Want to Start a Podcast

There are many reasons to have a podcast. You've gotten this far in wanting to learn how to launch and maintain your own podcast. Your voice matters and should be heard. Think through why you want to start a podcast. Ask yourself, *"Why does this story need to be told?"* and *"Why am I the one to tell it?"* It is imperative that you consider the core reasons behind your podcast. Think about the desire to share your content with the world. Are you a business owner who wants to use a podcast to share your expertise to gain new clients? Do you feel you have an insight into a subject that is unique and should be shared with the world? Do you want to use it as an audio blog to keep your friends and family up to date on a life goal you are working to achieve? For example, if you are running your first marathon or quitting your job to backpack across Europe you might want to share your experiences and growth so that others may find inspiration or helpful information if they are at a similar stage of life.

At the heart of the *"why"* is you. The why in your podcast is paramount to moving forward and further developing your idea. Think about

6

what this podcast means to you, why it is important that it is in the world. What is your true mission for this podcast? For example, the concept of my podcast is simple and straightforward – I interview musicians and then produce the interviews with snippets of their music into a feature piece on the band. There are plenty of music related podcasts out there, so why do I do it? What is my mission in executing this podcast every week? As a journalist I have always been interested in the stories behind the artist, what drives them, what they are interested in and how that informs the music or art that they make. It is imperative that I give them the platform and space to share their own insights and perspectives. I do that through asking thoughtful and thoroughly researched questions that few others have asked. By engaging in a real and informed conversation I am able to provide the space for emotive content that listeners want to hear and that the musicians want to share with their fans. I am also able to introduce people to music that I feel passionately about, that might not otherwise receive the spotlight in mainstream press. My mission is to provide the space for an artist to share themselves with an audience in a way few others allow.

What Should Your Podcast Be About?

You've made the effort to seek out this manual on how to create a podcast. More than likely you have an idea for a podcast. Deciding what you want your podcast to be about goes beyond the topic itself and pulls from the personal mission, as well as the goals you have for this podcast. It may seem like the topic and the "*about*" are one and the same, but the "*about*" is deeper and reaches to the core of why you are making a podcast.

Let's say the topic of your podcast is a weekly film review. Every week you and perhaps a guest breakdown your favorite new releases and offer critical insight into the films that didn't quite hit the mark in your opinion. The *"about"* here is not the films you are reviewing, or even why you are reviewing them. What needs to be considered is the overall reasoning behind what you are presenting. Is the goal to review anything or are you trying to add a new perspective to the dialogue because you have degrees in film and production? Or perhaps you are on the other side of the coin and think it is important to present a layman's view that the general public can relate to. It is also possible that your podcast isn't really about movie reviews, but merely a vehicle to present a larger idea or opinion.

Think about what your podcast is about in a larger overarching theme. If you are struggling, ask yourself these questions:

- What is the mission of this podcast?
- What are the goals of this podcast?
- What information do you want to convey?
- What is your elevator pitch for this podcast?
  - If you had to describe this podcast to someone in 3 or 4 sentences what would you say?

What Audience Do You Want to Reach?

Once you have that all straightened out there is another important component to tackle – **audience.** There are two types of audiences to acknowledge. Understanding what these audiences are and who you are directing your podcast towards will help you further home in on the "*what's*" and "*why's*" of your project.

The first audience to consider is the one you already have; this is called your "*built-in-audience.*" If you were to release a podcast tomorrow without marketing, ads, newsletter blasts etc.—who would listen to it? Depending on your own personal and professional community that can mean: friends, family, social media followers, clients, professionals in your network that share the same demographics as you. Basically, anyone you have already touched in your life. Make a list of who that is and be careful to only include what we've already talked about. It is not a wish list of who you *want* to listen to your podcast (that comes next).

Now is where you get to dream big. The second type of audience is the audience you want to attract. There is a specific audience for your podcast. Here are some general statistics to give you an idea of how many people are listening and who they are.

According to Marketing Land[2] in 2018, 44% of people have listened to a podcast and in 2019 that number jumped to 51%, pushing it just over the majority. 32% of that number listens monthly, up from 26 percent the previous year.

Male listeners are slightly higher at 36% than women at 29% and the age ranges typically fall between 12-55 years old. Weekly listeners are listening to 7 podcasts per week on average.

---

[2] https://marketingland.com/u-s-podcast-audiences-keep-growing-62-million-listening-weekly-258179

As podcast topic offerings and awareness increase these numbers will steadily climb.

With that knowledge you must narrow down the true "*who*" for whom this podcast is made. Who do you want to listen to this podcast? Who do you want to attract? The best way to answer these questions is to be thoughtful about who could benefit from your perspective and opinions. It is best to consider who is in the world out there and who should be listening to your podcast. Be realistic when you answer this question, however, and don't land on *everyone*. Not everyone is going to have the same interests or concerns as you. Demographics, age, income, ethnicity, life stage, are all things you need to think through.

If you have an idea of who you want to listen to your podcast, you need to also think about when and where they listen. That can help you understand how long to make your content.

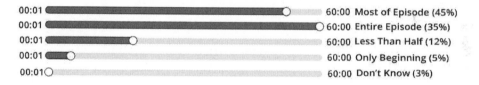

% of people listening to a complete podcast episode

Knowing where they listen helps inform how long your podcast should be and what kind of segments you should include. The majority of listeners listen to podcasts while doing other things. 26% have listened while driving. 11% while being at work. 4% while working out. And 3% while going for a walk.[3] So, if your podcast is geared towards stay-at-home parents you'll need to think about how that person likely has a lot going on while they are listening. Your content should be easy to engage with and listen to. Alternatively, if your target audience is a busy professional looking to get an edge up on their career, they likely have the bandwidth for a 30 minute straightforward and informative podcast they can listen to on their commute or while cooking dinner at home.

At home	In car/truck	At work	Riding public transportation	Working out	Walking around	Other
49%	22%	11%	4%	4%	3%	7%

Popular podcast listening areas and activities

How your audience listens to podcasts also needs to be taken into consideration as different distributors attract different listeners. Spotify is steadily becoming the most used player. They have heavily invested in podcasting as a platform with the acquisition of Gimlet Media and Anchor (a full-service podcast production and publishing software). Apple podcasts is still in the game, with Google podcasts, and Stitcher in the mix as well. We will talk more about the distribution options in chapter 7. Each of these platforms provides analytics, which you will have access to once your podcast is posted. You should be posting your podcast with all of these distributors, but

---

[3] Statistics from https://www.podcastinsights.com/podcast-statistics/

once you have access to the analytics, you'll be able to understand the best platform for your specific podcast. Then you can tailor future episodes and marketing campaigns based on which platforms get you the most listeners.

Once you have established these: your built-in-audience and the audience you want to listen you can tweak your podcast with them in mind. Attracting listeners is one thing, but maintaining them equates to success and you cannot maintain them if you do not know who this podcast is for beyond you.

2. Mapping Your Podcast

What is the Right Format for Your Podcast?

There are many format options for a produced podcast. Finding the right one for you can be as easy as mirroring an existing format or piecing together what makes sense for your concept. It is important to include music breaks between segments. It offers a reprieve from constant talking and gives your listeners an indicator that the subject is changing or a segment has ended and a new one is beginning. Most importantly, it relieves the brain from listening fatigue. There is also the option to use one or more of those breaks between segments to plug another show, highlight an advertisement, or include creative shorter content that does not warrant a longer segment, but is still important to your concept. A break like that could include reading a poem, a short reflective audio diary entry, or a fake commercial. You can come up with a format that makes sense for you and your content, which we will cover in Chapter 3 through storyboarding.

Being realistic about what is manageable for you in terms of a time commitment is a logistical key to success, the more segments you have the more time is spent in production. Similarly, if you have a podcast existing as one segment that is an hour-long conversation between you and a guest there could be a considerable amount of production time necessary to edit such a large block of audio.

It is important to think about how making a podcast fits into your schedule. How much time do you need to allow for scheduling guests, recording time, editing/production, writing the descriptions and show notes for each episode, and finally posting and promoting each episode. If you are hiring a producer to edit and mix your podcast, how much turnaround time do they need to complete the podcast and how does that impact your posting schedule? Be realistic about what you have time for and how you can provide quality content in a posting schedule that makes sense for your life.

What Style Should My Podcast be?

There are many styles of podcasts out there, and yours doesn't have to adhere to the already existing ones. You can be creative with how you format and map your content. Let's look at some examples of the more popular styles that are out there. If you'd like you can use these as a roadmap for your own.

The six main styles of podcasts in the world right now are:

1.) Interview

2.) Story-telling

3.) Repurposed content

4.) Mono-cast

5.) Educational

6.) Conversational

Interview podcasts feature one-on-one interviews as the main source of audio and are the most popular style of podcast out there. This type of podcast can feature many interviews in one episode or just one depending on the context and purpose. As a general rule in broadcast media, having two distinct voices present helps keep the brain engaged and reduces the chances of the audio sounding monotonous. Using interviews is the easiest way to solve that problem. Typically, an interview based show has a common thread in the host. As in, the guests on the show have some reason for being there which is provided by the host. For example, 'WTF With Marc Maron,' invites guests from all ranges of industries and disciplines, but the common denominator is Marc Maron. That isn't to say that you need to be a media personality to pull this style of podcast off. It just means that a conceptual thread is necessary for maintaining listeners. If you are introducing a new guest each week there has to be some sort of vision or overarching theme to the podcast itself to keep people tuning in.

Pros

- Minimal editing required in post-production due to the conversational nature.

- Guests provide valuable insight and their own content in addition to your questions, so you won't run out of things to say.

Cons

- More legwork in terms of scheduling guests.

- Interview podcasts are the most popular format out there, you'll need to make sure yours is different enough or niche enough for people to want to listen to it.

Story-telling podcasts have two genres, fiction and non-fiction. Both are heavily derived from Public Radio program format and often include narrative journalism. Narration is key with this style of podcast. There is a clear story being told through interviews, monologues, sometimes essays, and careful crafting of content. Criminal is one great example. Producing these types of stories is very labor intensive. Journalists will often record hours upon hours of tape to be produced down to a 25-minute story that will have you on the edge of your seat the entire time. If writing, researching, and storytelling comes naturally to you, this may be your style.

Pros

- Completely addicting to your audience, they'll always be coming back for more if you do it well.

- Tons of opportunity to be creative with production and how you tell the story.

Cons

- Audiences are expecting a very high production value with this type of show. It'll need to have a very professional sound, which means more work for you or a producer and potentially more money if you are hiring someone to help you produce.

- Lots of planning required to pull this off, research, interviews, writing, etc.

Repurposed content often comes from turning a live show into a podcast. Podcasts and programs like 'The Moth,' 'Prairie Home Companion,' and 'Wait, Wait, Don't Tell Me,' are all great examples.

These are live story telling shows, variety shows, and game shows of sort that have a mix of storytelling, musical performances and special guests appearing. They are recorded live and edited later so a larger audience can listen and participate in the fun. Let's say you host a comedy night or a special writer's open mic. You could record the shows and then add a podcast appropriate introduction and conclusion at the beginning and end of the show, clean up the breaks between acts and voilá, you have a podcast!

Pros

- Easy to record if you have a sound engineer already managing the sound for the show.

- Minimal editing required since it is already an hour-long event.

Cons

- More than likely, you'll need 2 recorders so you can record through the soundboard, but also record the audience in the room. It's not hard to sync those recorders, but it is an extra step to get a full-bodied sound to the podcast.

- Your live show might not be that engaging to an audience that can't see it, if it's not, you'll have to get creative with voice over to help your listeners along.

A **mono-cast** is a podcast which only has one voice, typically just the host. These podcasts consist of the host monologuing on a topic of their choosing. One that is important to them and probably something they are well versed in. Mono-casting offers the unique opportunity to showcase yourself and connect with your audience, who will more than likely feel as though they know you after just a few episodes. If mono-casting is for you, we'll go over best practices for how to do it in chapter 3.

<u>Pros</u>

- You are not on anyone else's schedule, so you can record whenever you have time or feel inspired.

- Your audience will become very invested in you specifically, which means a loyal listener base.

<u>Cons</u>

- You are responsible for any and all content – it is a one woman show after all.

Educational podcasts borrow formats from interviewing and conversational podcasts, but with a more directed approach. Since the purpose of an educational podcast is to provide a lesson of some sort, it is important for the segments to be structured and clear in the delivery of content. Take Malcom Gladwell's *'Revisionist History'* as an example. Each episode chooses an event, person, or idea from the past and re-presents it with the aim of getting to the true narrative knowing what we know now. For this style of podcast guests can be invited to lend their expertise in an interview format, but the goal should always be to teach the listener something on the subject at hand.

<u>Pros</u>

- Specific, intellectual content gives you easy structure and engages your listeners.

- Easier to maintain loyal audience.

- Supplemental content is a breeze to create. For example: pdf downloads, curriculum ideas, resource lists, courses, etc.

Cons

- You'll have to be creative in how you are *"teaching"* some content due to the inability to present visuals.

The last and quite popular style of podcasting is **conversational**. This one is often used because of its ease and usually includes two consistent hosts with an occasional guest. It is exactly as it sounds, as if two friends are carrying on a conversation. What makes it different from the interview style podcast is that there isn't one host asking questions of the second host for an hour. Rather each host is engaging with the other and the questions may go back and forth or they may just be sharing their opinions and discussing a topic without any questions at all.

Pros

- Only a brief outline is required rather than a lot of dedicated research and predetermined questions.

- You're not carrying the content alone, if you run out of things to say your partner can pick up the slack or help get you both back on track.

Cons

- You really have to concentrate on your niche here and make sure the topics you choose to discuss are things your audience wants to hear about.

- If your co-host lives elsewhere you'll have to do a little more editing to get the remote recorded tracks properly produced in post-production.

Sonic Feel

Another component that goes into further specifying the purpose and direction of the podcast is what it should sound like. There are many options for production and style out there. Choose one that is indicative of you. **Think about the sonic feel of your podcast**.

- When interviewing guests do you want it to feel comfortable and conversational or professional and straightforward?

- Do you want your voice to be front and center or are you more interested in presenting other people's perspectives without the distraction of your voice?

- What kind of tone do you want the podcast to have and what type of music will help provide that sound?

- What feeling do you want your music to convey? Upbeat? Funky? Meditative? Folky?

Listen to your favorite podcasts and make notes about what draws you in terms of how they sound. Then, consider the audience you are trying to reach. More than likely you've identified what your niche in the podcast community is going to be. Do everything in your power to feed that into your brand. If your podcast is light and educational, use a meditative or acoustic musical component. If your podcast is high energy and funny, add music or sound effects that continue that vibe throughout your segments. Think about what kinds of music your audience might already listen to. One way to figure out how to match your sonic feel to your target audience is by listening to the top podcasts in the genre you'll be publishing under. If your podcast falls under the *"self-improvement"* and *"fitness"* categories, look those genres up in apple podcast charts and listen to them.

How Frequently Do You Want to Release Your Podcast?

When deciding how frequently to release your podcast, there are two logistical decisions to make. First, you need to decide if you want your podcast to be a series (or serial) based podcast or an ongoing release.

Series podcasts function much like a television show. You would present on one topic or follow a narrative for a set number of episodes. Alternatively, if you do not want to release episodes throughout the year, then your podcast can happen seasonally. If this is the case, you can adhere to a three-month release schedule and then take a break until the next season. An ongoing release would mean that you are consistently releasing podcast episodes throughout the year using a specific posting schedule. Perhaps one of the most popular examples of a series podcast is *Serial* or *S Town*.

In the first season of *Serial* the journalist and host, Sarah Koenig investigates the 1999 disappearance of Hae Min Lee and the subsequent arrest of her ex-boyfriend Adnan Syed who was later sentenced to life in prison. Each episode attempts to get closer to the truth of what happened and how the trial misconstrued evidence. Fun fact, because of the attention from this podcast Adnan Syed's case and original trial are being reexamined.

The second decision is how often will you release your podcast? Popular formats are weekly, but you can also do daily, bi-monthly or every other week if you do not want to adhere to a monthly calendric model. Once a month is also an option, but it is not recommended for building a listener base. There is also the option to release all of your episodes at once for those who like to binge listen. This is only recommended if you have decided to go with the series or serial based podcast model.

Regardless of what you choose, the posting schedule should be adhered to consistently. Meaning podcasts should be released the same day each week or every other week. This allows you to build an audience base that will become familiar with when to listen to a new episode and also allows you time to build in your marketing plan. Choose a day of the week that is not heavily loaded with podcast releases. There is often a backlog of podcasts released for the Monday morning commute, which means you could get lost in the shuffle if you post on Friday-Sunday. Choosing a mid-week release time helps your listeners build you in as a habit and that maintains an audience.

The most important thing is that you are releasing quality episodes. While it may seem rigorous to stay on top of the newest trend or information, listeners will not listen to you if your work is poor or repetitive.

What is the Ideal Length for Your Podcast?

Having mapped out what type of content you'd like to provide and how often you plan to release episodes, now you have to decide how long your podcast episodes should be. They can range from ten to ninety minutes. Podcasts over an hour are not recommended. Most people do not have a dedicated block of time beyond an hour to listen to a podcast. As a reminder, some listen on their commute to work, while cooking dinner, or doing a task. The longer the podcast, the more consideration needs to go into keeping an audience engaged in your content.

Again, be realistic about your time and your audience's time. Really sit down and decide how much time you have to record, produce and publish. As far as your audience goes, remember who it is you are trying to attract and consider how much time they might be willing to give up of their life to listen to your episode.

For instance, if your audience are professionals or novices looking to learn something new, they are more than likely willing to listen to a 90 minute podcast once a month. If your audience is a network of backpackers following your epic travels hiking through Bali they'll likely give you 30 – 60 minutes of their time to find out what you're up to.

The topic helps to inform the length as it pertains to an audience as well. If you are talking about a current event your listener's attention span is short at 10-15 min. If you are breaking down a complicated topic into many segments and perspectives they'll likely give you 60 minutes. Just make sure your episode is engaging. Once someone turns a podcast off, they are unlikely to return to it.

The general rules of thumb for podcasting releases are:

Frequency	Duration
Daily	*10-15 min*
Weekly or Bi-Monthly	*60 min*
Monthly	*90 min*

When trying to figure out the logistics of how to arrive at the length of your episode, some helpful things to acknowledge are the lengths of each segment. Generally speaking, if you are monologuing you want that segment to fall between ten to fifteen minutes. That may seem like a short time but speaking for fifteen minutes straight outside of conversation is hard and needs to be well thought out to keep someone listening. A conversation or interview style segment should be kept around the twenty-minute mark after post-production. You may speak with someone for much longer but some of the fluff of the conversation can be taken out. Audiences don't need to hear the first five to ten minutes of warm up. Additionally, some questions or conversation topics might fall flat and should be taken out to prevent a listener from losing interest.

It is recommended that music breaks remain short, between fifteen and thirty seconds. They are meant to signal a new topic or segment is coming and act as a transition. If a music break is too long you run the risk of lost interest or a listener forgetting what the previous segment was about before moving into the next one. It is important to allow enough time for the brain to naturally adjust to this shift in audio, but as a rule of thumb music does not need to take up that much time in a podcast. It is mainly used to reduce listening fatigue. Once you sketch out how much time you need for each segment and allow for music breaks, you'll have a rough estimate of how long your podcast will be.

Segment	Duration
Intro w/ music bed	*1-2 min*
1 segment of monologuing	*15 min*
Music break	*15-20 seconds*
1 interview	*20 min*
Music break	*15-20 seconds*
Extra short segment	*5 min*
Music and Outro	*1 min*

This is around 42 minutes, so your podcast is under an hour but longer than 30 minutes.

3. How to Bring Your Content to Life

How to Make Effective Introductions

When crafting your content, the easiest thing start with is your **intro and outro**. These are generally pre-recorded and mixed with music so they can be dropped at the beginning and end of your podcast. Including music in your intros and outros locks in your listener and sets the tone for the entire episode. It also acts as a way to solidify your brand in the podcast. Using the same snippet of music for the intro and outro acts as a sort of theme music. If you don't want to pre-record your intros and outros you just have to remember to include them while you are recording your episode and add the music fade ins and outs in post-production. There are a couple types of introductions that need to be in each episode.

The first is general and explains what the podcast is - who you are (or the hosts), maybe why you are making this podcast, what it aims to do, what people can expect etc. This intro will be included at the beginning of every episode you publish and can/should be recorded ahead of time.

"I'm Amanda Mayo and you're listening to Native Growth, a podcast about bringing native flora to lawns across America. Each week I travel to a different region of the U.S. and speak with homeowners who are doing their part to rehabilitate their little pieces of earth by planting native flora. We cover a detailed description of the plants native to the region, the benefits to the land and how they impact the natural

ecosystem. Follow along for tips and tricks and general plant nerd knowledge!"

The second intro should specifically introduce the episode, who you'll be speaking with, and what you'll be covering. This one can be pre-recorded and dropped in during production, or you can speak it while recording your first segment.

"This week on Native Growth I'm in Illinois where a group of neighbors in a suburb of Chicago have banded together to make their block look like the prairies that used to roll as far as the eye could see in what is now Oak Park. You may know Oak Park as the home of the influential architect Frank Lloyd Wright who was known for his natural architecture and prairie style homes. In this episode we highlight the plants that were once prevalent in the area and what their jobs were to this ecosystem. I'll speak with Mary and John Smith who started the movement in their neighborhood to make their front yard look like a prairie and we'll hear from some locals and what they think about all of this happening in their own front yards!"

Now that might look like a lot of text, but if you speak it out loud and time yourself, you'll see it will translate to mere seconds of tape. It's important to know what you want to say in your introductions, scripting is fine, but keep in mind it should have the tone of your speaking voice. Think of it like you're explaining to a friend how an evening you have planned for them is going to proceed. It shouldn't sound like you are reading it. Don't worry too much about it being correct on the page in terms of grammar or reading flow. Instead use it as an opportunity to let your listeners know what to expect from both your podcast and a specific episode.

The outros should follow similar guidelines, but in reverse order. The first outro should quickly state what your next episode is about and thank listeners for joining you.

"Thanks for joining me in Oak Park on this episode of Native Growth! Next week I head a little North to Wisconsin where forest life and underbrush once prevailed. For information found in this episode refer to the show notes or visit the native growth podcast [dot] com."

The more general pre-recorded outro should include links to your social media, website, and anything else that is relevant to this particular podcast. This will run at the end of every episode, no matter the content.

"Get your native plant fix every week by subscribing to Native Growth wherever you get your podcasts! Want to see photos of the beautiful flora we discuss? Follow us on Instagram [at] Native Growth Podcast and as always if you have any questions or would like to be featured on our show send us a note via the contact form on our website. Until next time plant nerds!"

How to Interview and Make Your Guests Comfortable

If you are **interviewing** a guest as part of your podcast there are many things to take into account to get good tape. What makes a good interview? **Perspective**. In any interview, it's your job to gather the facts and report them to your audience. But it's also your job to gather perspectives from different people and use their quotes (in this case, tape) to tell the story.

The first step towards preparing for your interview is **pre-interviewing + research**.

Preparing. Do background research on your subject. Knowing a little about what they do, where they work, or the history of a subject will help you formulate questions.

Research. Do a relatively in depth Google search and note the stories they've told previously, or what information is already out there and has been repeated. You'll want to cover some of this with your interviewer but it is best to frame it into a question that might result in different information rather than having them just spout off what they've told every other press outlet repeatedly.

Ask ahead of time. If there are things you'd like to know that are not readily available on the internet you may e-mail them a list of questions. This is called *"pre-interviewing"* and will save time during the interview so you can summarize some of the basics and not make them re-tell their origin story on tape *or* it will give you an idea of what to ask and how to frame it. You can also use this opportunity to ask them if there is anything they'd like you to ask them about - this can inform the arc of your interview.

Know what you want to know. Before you go into an interview, think about what information and ideas you need to gather in order to complete your story. It sounds simple, but it's the most important step to a good interview.

Before you sit down to interview someone make a list of questions. Come with a basic list of questions - seven questions typically results in twelve minutes of tape. You don't need to make a list of every single thing you want to know or every question that you might want to ask.

Jot down basic ideas you need to cover and any important questions you don't want to forget. Working with an outline of ideas and conversation starter questions is helpful.

It does depend on how much time you want to allow for the interview. If you have an hour you can be more conversational. If you only have fifteen minutes with someone, you want to use that time wisely to engage in the questions you really want answered. In this case you'd want a list of questions to pull from rather than a general outline.

Great quotes often come out of an interview that doesn't seem as formal and is more conversational. If you're not completely comfortable, make a list of questions to pull from, but don't be afraid of poignant silence as well. Sometimes interviewees need time to formulate their thoughts and expand on what they've just said.

How to make guests comfortable...

Even if you know your guest intimately it is important to remember that everyone takes some time to adjust to having a microphone or equipment in their face. You are the host and therefore, are in control, so it is your job to make them feel comfortable and guided. I recommend starting by explaining what you are doing. More than likely they know why they are there, to be interviewed for a podcast! Sometimes, like in the case of interviewing a musician or important figure who gets a lot of press recognition, they might not know why they are there or what this is for.

Say something like *"Just to let you know this is an audio recording that will later be used for a podcast. It will be edited so if you'd like to restate something you've said that is completely fine!"*

And

"My podcast is called 'x' and I cover these topics. We will be talking for about ten minutes depending on how the conversation goes."

I recommend giving these introductions while you are setting up your equipment or taking levels. This gives them time to adjust to the equipment's presence and it also centers everyone (yourself included) for the interview itself. It creates the space for the interview and acts as a natural transition into the start of the interview, rather than jumping into recording immediately and asking a question.

To further loosen up, ask a silly or easy to answer question while you are adjusting your levels for the interview itself. We will go over how to record in Chapter 6, but keep this in mind. Asking something like, *"What did you have for breakfast this morning?"* gives them something easy to think about and likely enough of an answer for you to gather the appropriate levels. You can also ask something humorous like, *"What is your favorite color of skittle?"*

What to ask and what *NOT* to ask...

Cover the 5 W's. Make sure you understand the who, what, where, when, why of the story at hand. With an expert interview this may relate to the person's professional background and research. Asking these types of interrogative questions allow the person or people you're interviewing to provide a narrative response.

Don't ask yes or no questions. Again, see the 5 W's. Yes or no questions will leave you with short, unusable answers. The only time it is appropriate to ask a yes or no question is if you need to fact check something in the moment because you don't have the research handy.

31

For example, a date, or year or person's name etc. That can be removed later in post, just remember to rework their answer into the form of a question.

Don't ask leading questions. Your questions shouldn't put words in a person's mouth or assume how they feel. Don't ask something like, *"Don't you feel upset about this?"* Instead, ask them how they feel about something and let them respond. Generally speaking, you have already formulated an idea of their work or the story at hand so be careful not to involve your own perspective in the question you are asking. It is important to get their perspective over yours.

Don't waste time on questions that you can easily find answers to. For example, rather than, *"What's the name of your new book?"* ask, *"I read that your new book, 'Homegrown,' was named after the small town where you grew up. What made you want to pay that tribute to your hometown?"* Rather than asking, "When does the book tour start?" try, *"It looks like the tour you're starting next week will keep you on the road for two months. How do you adjust to life on the road when you're away that long?"* or *"You're heading to Europe on this book tour, hitting half a dozen countries over the course of three weeks. How do you deal with the language barriers and culture shock of traveling to so many countries in such a short a time?"*

Similarly, don't waste time asking them something that you can summarize for them. For example, when introducing a guest don't say *"I'm here with Sarah Mills; Sarah, please tell our listeners a little bit about what you do."* If you do that you will more than likely get a longer response than is necessary, or they might clam up and not want to sing their own praises. Instead, introduce them for your listeners in a quick and concise way, *"I'm here with Sarah Mills, a marine biologist currently working on climate change research through studying a little-known oceanic organism called the blah blah. Her ground-breaking research has paved a new path forward on how to reverse climate change."* This way also helps lead you into your first question, *"Thank you for joining me today Sarah."* Allow her to answer with thanks and praise and then move into your conversation, *"What would you say is the most important thing we need to know about this organism you are studying?"*

Get your information in small chunks. Avoid multiple questions at once or huge questions that are too open-ended. Rather than finding your way to a question on mic, ask questions from your list and formulate new questions in your head while the interviewee(s) answer. If you have a question that is three-pronged, your guest will forget what the first two questions were by the time you have finished, or they will have formulated a response to the first question in the time it has taken you to ask the other two, and therefore didn't even hear your other questions. Instead, break it up into one general question with two more specific follow up questions.

"Tell me about...." If you don't know what to ask, *"Tell me about...."* is a great way to gather information. This is particularly helpful for interviews where you don't have a lot of time to prepare beforehand, or for when you want the interview subject to get out from behind the details and give you some perspective. It is also helpful to use this if they mention something that catches your attention, but you aren't sure what to ask in the moment.

Asking the emotional questions. Part of getting perspective is getting a person's opinions and emotions. Asking questions like, *"How do you feel about this?"* or *"What were you thinking when this happened?"* are good for helping people talk about experiences. If you're talking to someone about an issue, plainly ask them *"Why*

33

should we care?" You'll more than likely get a response with great emotional perspective.

You are not the story: You are there to talk to the person(s), not about yourself. It's not about you, it's about them. You might relate a personal point as a way to get into a question, but your interviewee(s) should be doing most of the talking.

During the interview...

Make eye contact. While the person is talking, try to look at them and respond to what they're saying - do this with NON-VERBAL cues, without making any sound, use nods or facial expressions. Making eye contact will make the interview feel less like a firing squad and more like a conversation.

Think about when you are on the phone with someone and you both speak at the same time, neither party can hear what the other said. It works the same way on tape. If you speak over them with an *"oh yes,"* or *"great,"* or *"uh huh,"* the listener is unable to hear what they have said. Practice using non-verbal cues in your daily life and that will help you integrate the practice into your recording process.

Listen. Sometimes we're so wrapped up in asking the questions that we forget to listen to the answers. PAY ATTENTION TO WHAT THEY SAY AND NOT WHAT YOU EXPECT THEM TO SAY. Engage with the person you are interviewing and listen carefully to what they say. You may want to make a note if you hear something that prompts a follow-up question.

Ask them to repeat something important. Sometimes a noise will interrupt your interview or your subject will trail off after an important idea, ruining a great piece of tape. Don't be afraid to ask that person to repeat themselves. It might seem awkward, but it's much worse to come away with bad tape.

Keep them on the mic. Don't let a whole interview go by where someone is off-mic. It's OK to ask someone to get back on the mic and repeat something they said previously.

Interrupt them. Don't be afraid to stop them from rambling, it is not offensive to re-state the question to re-direct them. You have given them the opportunity to organize their thoughts on the matter.

Ending the interview

Ask one of two final questions:

"Is there anything else that I haven't asked that you think I should know for this interview?"

This is good for stories with a lot of details where I'm new to the subject and may not have thought to ask about something important.

OR

"Of all the things we've talked about today, what do you think is the most important piece of information that you want our listeners to understand?"

Great for rambling, wonky interviews where you're afraid you didn't get any good tape. Often people who were boring for 15 minutes will pull it together for one usable quote.

Thank them and get further information. Such as social media handles and website. Be sure to either say this on the recording yourself or have them say it, this will point your listeners to where they can get further information about your guest and it will also serve as a documented record for you in the event that you cannot find their website or social handles through a search later on.

How to Write a Script

If your podcast includes segments with just you speaking, that is called monologuing or voice over (VO). Depending on your personality you might love the idea of speaking unscripted for twenty minutes to no one in particular on a mic, or you might be terrified by this! Even if you are the type of person that is comfortable talking to yourself, you should still have an outline to work with, no one wants to hear you ramble for an extended period of time while you search for the thing you really want to be saying.

There are a couple ways to build an outline. You can sketch out larger ideas and themes you'd like to touch on in a certain order, as you would when outlining a long paper. If you are not an academic thinker, however, and need prompts to get going you can interview yourself. Jot down questions and then just answer them on tape. When you use this format, it is helpful to remember to include the content of the question in the answer, for example, "*why am I making this podcast?*" Answer, "*I am making this podcast because....*"

Be sure to include key words or phrases that you know you want to mention. Dates, names, resources, a current event you are referencing etc. those types of things should make it into your outline. Below I'm

36

providing an example. My podcast is about music and the first segment includes me reviewing a new release and discussing why I like a band.

- **Album Review: Lowland Hum, Glyphonic** released 2018 on Tone Tree Music *(10 min)*
  - My rank: 9 out of 10
    - Departure from usual sound.
    - Cohesive album as compared to *Thin (2017) + Native Air (2013).*
  - First attempt at a non-linear storytelling album.
  - Used folk tradition blended with new techniques to achieve a scenic backdrop.
  - Wrap up – evolution of sound, production quality, and storytelling.
- **Transition**
- **Why I love this Band** *(10 min)*
  - They provide emotional access to their music.
    - Hashtag Support Quiet Music.
    - Concerts in the Blind.
    - Lyric Books at live shows.
  - Cite reddit thread of fans discussing live shows with lyric books.
  - Other bands involved in hashtag supportquietmusic.

o Conclusion – involvement in larger music community, consideration of listeners and audience, how that comes across in their music.

Another option for voice over is to write yourself a script to read, like you would for your intro and outro. Write like you speak so it sounds natural and not like you are reading something. Consider that one hundred words is about a minute of tape. If your segment needs to be twenty minutes, that is a fair amount of text to write out. Using active voice will help keep listeners engaged. It will feel unnatural at first to record yourself reading a script. Be mindful to include pauses like you would in a conversation. Pause when you have completed an idea or make an important point. This gives the listener time to absorb what you have said. Read the script out loud a couple of times before you record. You'll be able to adjust the writing for flow and practice any pronunciations that may be difficult.

Remember to set the scene in your script. You want your listener to feel immersed in what you are saying and the story you are telling. Not to the extent of *"on a dark and stormy night,"* but you could let them know where you are and what's going on around you if it's important to your story. In that same vein, choose language that is descriptive when you're talking about something specific. Help the listener visualize it. For example, if you are telling a story about someone who has an irrational fear of grocery shopping, paint that picture for your listener.

Instead of: *When Ron walks into a grocery store, he is overwhelmed with anxiety and it's very hard for him to complete his shopping.*

Try: *As Ron approaches the grocery store his steps become more labored, as if walking through cement. Once inside, his chest begins to tighten as he gazes out into the sea of produce. He is paralyzed by the 3 rows filled with dozens upon dozens of cartons containing different varieties of apples. Red, green, red and green, yellow, gold, he can't even remember if he likes apples.*

A script should be a combination of an outline and a written script. You don't want it to sound like you are reading. Leave room for inspiration and improvisation. If this is a topic you are discussing, chances are you've done the research and are well versed on the subject. Trust that you can speak about it clearly with a little help from a script. It is helpful to write out your introduction, transitions, and conclusions so you don't get stuck trying to talk yourself into the next phase. Here's an example of how to do that.

Welcome back to PSYCHED! This season we are talking about people's irrational fears and what that might mean in terms of psychology. On today's episode I'm tackling the elusive but not as you might think, fear of grocery shopping! Let me set the scene for you, our protagonist is Ron. He HATES grocery shopping, but not for the usual reasons. He hates it because he's terrified of it.

- Talk about how Ron feels when he walks into a grocery store.

You may be wondering why he's feeling this way, why the rational mind has decided to take a back seat, letting anxiety and fear run rampant. According to the Psychiatry Monthly Journal on Anxiety

- 1 in 100 people suffer from irrational fears regarding shopping.
- The root cause is unknown but can be tied to issues of control.
- More data.

- Analyze how Ron fits into the criteria.

Those statistics combined with Ron's situation may seem grim, but there is hope for Ron yet! The solution is quite simple.

- Definition of irrational fear: A persistent, abnormal, and irrational fear of a specific thing or situation that compels one to avoid it, despite the awareness and reassurance that it is not dangerous.

- What worked for others in a similar situation.

- Meditation, talk therapy, immersion therapy.

- Support system – now he brings a friend with him to keep him calm.

Now that Ron is aware of his fear and has taken steps to treat it, he is able to grocery shop on his own without anxiety.

- Paint picture of what that looks like now vs before.

- Benefits – spending less money, buying what he actually needs, cooking more, healthier existence.

Once again psychology gives us the solutions to some of life's hardest curveballs. Of course the disclaimer is, these solutions don't work for everyone. How fascinating to know you may not be alone if you have an irrational fear of grocery shopping. Be sure to reach out to a therapist or friend if you find the techniques in this podcast didn't work for you. I'd also love to hear from you either way! [At] me on Twitter [at] psyched podcast.

Thanks for joining me today on Psyched! Next week we'll dive into everyone's favorite, the irrational fear of spiders!*

*none of the statistics or research cited above is real, I made it up to show an example of how to write a script.

Whether you choose to go the route of an outline or a script it is important to repeat the information you are sharing often and clearly. Unlike a book where someone can highlight something important or go back to read it, audio can often go in one ear and out the other. It will feel redundant to you, but often a listener will not have *heard* the important point or reference you are making the first or even second time.

Pro-tip: don't trail off at the end of a sentence! The last word is just as important as the first.

Now, go and test it out. Record yourself telling your friend a story or have them sit in with you while you record a monologue. Listen back and pay attention to the language you used. This is particularly helpful if you are having a hard time writing like you speak, which can be more difficult than you might think. Take note of which words come naturally to you and how you are talking throughout the story. Think back on what you left out and what you put an emphasis on when re-telling your tale. Then, observe when your friend was most engaged in your story. How did they react, when did they react? etc. This practice round will help you build and tighten up your script.

How to Structure Your Content Using Storyboarding

Once you have decided on your podcast's content, format, and the logistics of releasing it you need to know how to structure your content. Regardless of if you are working in a series-based podcast or an ongoing one, a plan must be devised for each episode. Audiences will not listen to a meandering host.

Storyboarding is extremely important to produce a successful podcast for many reasons. It will provide you with a concrete outline of what each episode needs, what content you need to gather, and who you need to speak to in order to round out the story. Having the episodes outlined provides a clearer picture of how to gather your content. It gives your podcast overall consistency, establishes the arch of the flow, and organizes your content into something your audience actually wants to listen to. It also gives you a general overview of how your episodes go together.

Storyboarding can also help you track audience engagement. Your hosting site will provide statistics. Using storyboarding, you can measure those statistics and audience feedback as it relates to the organization of your content. You will be able to see which episodes were most successful. When paired with your storyboarding method and listener feedback you can easily deduce what parts of your content and flow your audience is gravitating towards.

There are many options out there to help you storyboard. You can use something like Asana - a project management tool, a mind mapping software, or a good old-fashioned table or spreadsheet. Below I have outlined the way we do it in radio. As you solidify the style that works best for you, this process will be a breeze.

Outline a sample episode or story.

You can do this however you'd like (on a whiteboard, with sticky notes, etc.), although it can help to brainstorm out loud with a partner first. Treat this like a draft or a sketch, don't get stuck in details. You will iron out and finalize as you go.

Begin with a more general approach to the content itself and what you are covering in the episode.

Use these discussion prompts as needed:

- What is the story's premise? Is it supported by pre-interviews, reporting, science, etc.?
- Is there enough depth to the story to sustain the length you've envisioned?
- What essential story elements do you need?

Consider: character(s), conflict/problem, setting, universal theme / idea that rises above the story, etc.

- Does this story have a central question? Can you ask it in one sentence?
- How does this story help fulfill your overall concept?
- How does this story serve your audience and its needs (as defined previously)?

Once you've answered those questions, try these activities:

- List the essential ingredients you need to make the best story (such as: reporting and information, voices, scenes, etc.).
- Story map and/or storyboard the piece to figure out its narrative arc.

- Describe the potential format. For example, is it scripted narrative, loose, unscripted, or non-narrated?

- If there is a host/narrator, what does that person do and how do they sound?

Further tighten up your storyline:

- List things the story is not about.

- What rabbit holes should you avoid?

- What subjects will take you off topic?

- What aspirations are unrealistic?

Let's say my podcast is about breaking down the barriers between Fine Art and the public. I've decided on 3 segments and a 45 min long podcast. I typically like to use sticky notes and stick them to the wall inside a masking tape table, which gives me the freedom to move it around. After answering all of the questions above and landing on how I'm going to structure my episode, I put it in a table so it can exist in digital form for easy reference and archival purposes. Here's an example of the end product.

Barriers of Art Podcast Ep 5 – The Museum

Central question: *Is a visitor really able to discern the intention of the artwork when it is installed in a museum?*

Format: *Unscripted interviews, conversational, with a touch of narration.*

Not About: *the meaning of art, whether or not a piece is good or bad, if the piece stands on its own without explanation, and pleasing everyone.*

	Segment 1	Segment 2	Segment 3
What	**Public Perspective**	**Artist Perspective**	**Museum Perspective**
Story Elements	Go to a museum, pick a piece of contemporary work and interview people's: 1.) Interpretations, reactions, and thoughts. 2.) Additional tape of me narrating what the work is, reading the informational panel, and describing the set up in the museum.	Interview the artist about the piece. 1.) Find out the deeper meaning behind it 2.) How they considered public interaction with it 3.) What they have done to ensure the public understands the work.	Talk to curator and/or programs manager to find out: 1.) Why they choose to display that work 2.) What they did to help the public understand it 3.) What the response has been like 4.) What supplemental programs have been put in place to educate visitors.
Purpose	Provide insight from real	Understand the true intention	Gain insider information on

	members of the public	behind the work.	how museums think about art-
Avoid	Is it good or bad art? What is art?	Steer clear of the, *"I can't control what anyone sees in my work"* approach.	Providing my perspective on what works and what doesn't.

Keeping the organizational approach in mind, it is also helpful to note that there are a several different types of storytelling. You may be unaware of how often these four are used so pay attention the next time you listen to a podcast or watch a television show. Having this knowledge can help you choose the best approach for sharing the information you want to share o your podcast.

First there is **chronological storytelling**. This type of story is exactly as it sounds it tells the events as they unfold in the order they happened. It will always include a beginning, middle, and end. Using my *Barriers of Art* podcast as an example the bones of the story would go something like this:

At Rachel Doe's studio we learn everything there is to know about the work of art we're discussing. She tells us how she came to show this work in the museum. At the museum we find out what they loved about her work and what they've done to ensure the public understands the intention behind the work. Talking with visitors gives us the truth behind whether the artist and museum succeeded in their efforts to help the public understand the artwork.

Second is **circular narrative**. This type of narrative ends in the same place it began. This type of story makes the big reveal at the beginning and then cycles through the events that actually result in the conclusion. This is great for stories that have a big hook as knowing the outcome helps keep the listener engaged and wanting to know more about how that happened. A lot of crime shows use this format, opening with the crime itself and then going back to the beginning to explain what happened. As an example, the flow of my podcast in a circular narrative would look something like this:

Open with visitor testimonial explaining the meaning of the piece in front of them. Follow chronological story of visiting artist's studio, speaking with museum staff, and then end on a different visitor explaining their perspective.

The third type of storytelling is **broken narrative**. Here, the narrative is broken up by providing context to all of the actions in the story. It can follow a chronological order, but what makes it a broken narrative is the addition of context. Building on the crime show archetype, let's say the crime is a run of the mill break in. Nothing was stolen, but clearly the robbers were looking for something. The break in the narrative could flash back to earlier that day when the owner discovered his grandfather had passed and left him a large sum of cash hidden under a mattress. Since the banks were not open yet, he brought it with him to work to hide it in a safe under the floorboards that only he knew about. His jealous cousin followed him to the store but was unable to see where the cash had been hidden. Then you'd flash forward to resume the story with the cousin hiring a team of robbers to break into the store when the owner left for lunch. The way I would use broken narrative in my podcast would be:

Interviewing the artist about their work, they say something specific about what they expect the public to feel when they look at the piece. I'd then cut to a real visitor at the museum explaining just that. When we move on to interviewing the museum, I'd use that same technique to interweave the artist's words or the visitor's words to either debunk the museum's philosophy or reinforce that it was successful.

The last storytelling format is the simplest. I suggest starting with this one if you are stuck or too in your head about how to format your ideas. The **three-act storytelling** method comes from theater and has been around for centuries. It is illustrated below in Fig2:

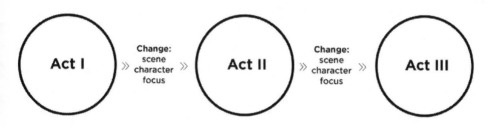

The idea is that you have 3 things to work with and 3 acts to do it in. The three things are scene, character, and focus. All you have to do is choose one to focus on for the first act, then change to a different one in the second act, and whatever is left is what the third act becomes about. If you choose to describe your character in the first act, then you would change to setting the scene in the second act, and wrap up with the focus of the story in act three. It doesn't matter what you choose or what order you choose to go in, just that you are choosing a different thing each time. This shift in the focus of the story keeps audiences engaged and interested. I choose to use this method of storytelling in my original table above.

The first act is where I set the scene at the museum with the people who the story is really about. The second act we change gears and get to know the artist as a character. In the last act I change the focus to the museum, the true reason and focus for the entire episode. The institution is the reason we are there, they brought all of these parties together. So I end by shifting the focus towards a conclusion.

Applying any of these storytelling methods to your content is a surefire way to make and keep your listeners engaged. They are tried and true for a reason.

Scheduling Your Podcast and Guests

As previously discussed in Chapter 2 scheduling your podcast is an important factor in managing your time and posting schedule. Now that you have storyboarded your episodes and general goals for the podcast you can figure out when to schedule guests and how much time to allow for production. See Chapter 6 for a complete explanation of production timelines.

It is good practice to always be working on more than one episode at a time. Until you get the hang of the workflow it is a good idea to have three episodes done and produced before you even post your first. This gives you lead time to produce and post the rest as it adheres to your previously decided upon posting schedule.

When scheduling guests you'll need to figure out location. If you are able to meet in person, are you going to them or are they coming to you? How long does it take for either one of you to get to the agreed upon location? If you are doing a remote interview, what kind of time zone compatibility are you dealing with? This is why it is particularly helpful to figure out what your episodes will include ahead of time. The physical logistics of an interview will determine when it is best to conduct an interview. There is no need to interview guests in the order of your episodes. If it works better for everyone's schedule to interview a guest for episode 5 now, then you can do that and just save the tape for when it is time to produce that episode.

It is always best to work backwards from a posting deadline. Depending on the length of your podcast and the number of segments included, production can take anywhere from one to seven days. You'll want to be sure and schedule your guest far enough in advance of when you are turning your tape over to a producer. If you are producing it yourself then you'll know your limits and how much time you'd need to dedicate to getting it out on time.

In general, it is good practice to interview someone one to two weeks before you go into production. This allows for changes as needed. Things come up on either your end or theirs and building in that time provides a buffer if someone needs to cancel or reschedule.

4. Who are the best Collaborators for Your Podcast?

Should I have a Co-Host?

Your subject matter will help determine what makes the most sense for the delivery of your content. Getting other people involved can really liven up your message. You can do that through a co-host, interviews with guests, and even conversations with multiple people or a panel. You can also interview people and completely remove yourself from the conversation in post-production – allowing the interviewee to shine through in totality.

Adding a co-host can enhance the listener's experience. Co-hosting is a great prerogative to make your podcast more enjoyable for you and your audience. The opportunity for riffing off one another and including banter keeps people engaged. It also helps the audience hear more of your personality as you interact with one another. It is important to choose the right co-host, however, just because you and your bestie have a great relationship and rapport, that doesn't necessarily mean they are the best option. You know that saying, "*You should never live with your best friend if you want them to stay your best friend?*" Co-hosting is similar because you are committing to a relatively permanent arrangement, so you need to be careful of who you choose. Some things to think about when deciding on your co-host:

1.) Are they reliable?

- As you may have gathered by now, podcasting is time consuming and consistent hard work needs to be applied to make it a success. Make sure your co-host is equally as invested and will show up.

2.) Do you have chemistry AND knowledge?

- Chemistry is great, you should absolutely be able to riff off one another and have a witty rapport to keep listeners interested, but you should not rely solely on that to carry you through each episode. Make sure you both have knowledge and insight that is sustainable for the vision of your podcast.

3.) Are the two of you the best fit for your audience?

- It is important to remember that for the most part, no one cares about two friends having a chat with a bunch of inside jokes in it. Just because you two think you're funny and share comedic antidotes, that doesn't mean your audience will also find you humorous. Be sure you can stay on topic; in a sense you are there to do a job for your audience, not waste their time with meaningless banter.

Have you got yourself a co-host? Great. Now, how to work with them to make your show the best show it can be! This first tip also applies to interviews.

1.) Use your non-verbal ques.

- Establish a non-verbal language with each other by using hand signals or gestures, body language, and facial expressions to keep each other engaged and communicating without having to speak. DO NOT TALK OVER EACH OTHER, no matter how excited you get!

2.)   Plan ahead.

- Have a meeting to discuss what you will be covering in your next episode and divide the work equally so you each have a stake in the episode. This also ensures you are not fumbling for what to say or where to go with your conversation.

3.)   Focus on your co-host.

- Theoretically you are both in the spotlight as hosts, but try not to think about it that way. Think about it in terms of helping the other person shine, if you both do that for each other you are guaranteed to have a great conversation.

Guests for Interviews

If your content requires interviews as part of your podcast, you'll need to know how to identify the best fit for your episodes and the most professional way to reach out to a person. Having gone through the storyboarding for each episode you should have an idea of what topics you'd like to discuss with a potential guest. If you are just starting out you should start with people you know who are willing to speak with you on tape. A professional contact or someone who you share an interest on the topic at hand with would work just fine. As you grow your audience and your reach you can begin to ask more of the people you may have had in mind.

I like to start with a list as I am storyboarding, so that way I know who I would like to speak with throughout the season of my podcast. This is also helpful if some of the guests you'd like to invite on your show are not local to where you live. You can start the process of communication with them to find out if they are going to be in your area in the near future. It is also helpful in regards to scheduling because you can conduct the interviews when it make sense and then leave them in the can for when you need them for an episode even if it's months down the line.

Cast a net to your own network asking for recommendations on people they think you should interview. This gives you a starting point to do some research on who they come back with to figure out if they are a good fit. If someone sends you a great candidate, ask them for an intro. People are always more willing to speak to someone when there is a mutual acquaintance involved.

Another way to scope out potential guests is by attending events that align with the subject matter of your podcast. More than likely you're already doing this so make sure you have a business card or postcard with you to hand out. Include the show page and a short blurb about the podcast as well as your contact information. Start talking to people face to face to let them know about your podcast. Save the interview pitch for e-mail or phone later, use this opportunity to get them interested in what you're already doing.

Something else to consider is whether or not someone would make a good guest. It's hard to know this if your intended interviewee is not in the public eye and has not done other interviews that you can watch or listen to. If you've had the opportunity to meet them, however, pay attention to how the speak, if they are engaging and happy, or even funny. I've been fortunate enough to interview some of my absolute favorite people and a couple of idols, but they are not always good on tape. Sometimes people just don't have the best affect for answering questions in a way that is engaging for a listener. It's not always a reason *not* to interview someone, but if you know this ahead of time you can better prepare for short and direct answers from your guest. You'll just have to do a little more work to make them comfortable and willing to have a real conversation with you.

If you haven't met them and there are no interviews out in the world with them, how can you find this out ahead of time? The best way is through pre-interviewing, which we covered in Chapter 3. After your initial pitch, send them a list of questions to vet them. If their answers are super short and not interesting, you'll know you need to rethink the way you're asking the questions. If they give you great, non-rambling answers they'll likely be a good person to interview.

There are a couple of ways you can initiate contact if you don't have an in with someone. You can message a potential guest on social media. If you do this a simple *"Hi I'm Amanda and host of music podcast at WXPR, I'd love to talk to you about being on the show! Can we discuss over email?"* When inviting a guest to be on your show be professional, courteous, and brief. Via e-mail, explain in a couple sentences who you are and what your podcast is about. Let them know you know about their work and ask them if they would be interested in coming on your show.

- Start by making sure your subject line is interesting and eye catching, so it doesn't get deleted without being opened.

- Explain who you are and what your credentials are, but be brief. No one wants to read a novel. Here's an example: Dear Tom, I'm a Music Director at WXPR. I've written for NPR,

Consequence of Sound, and Pitchfork as a music writer and now I use my talents to host WXPR's weekly music podcast.

- Give them information about the podcast itself, again be concise. Each week we feature an up and coming musician and invite a music critic or expert to give their thoughts. This is then mixed together with music into a feature piece that runs on our podcast.

- Make the ask and include next steps. I've always admired your knowledge of the scene and saw that you recently wrote a piece about the musician we are featuring next. Would you be interested in being interviewed on the show? Typically interviews last 20 minutes and we either conduct them in the studio or by direct phone-in. Let me know if you have any questions and are available and I'll get the ball rolling!

Be prepared to answer follow-up questions. Depending on the person's reach or if you are going through a PR person, here is a list of potential things they might like to know in their response to you:

- How many listeners you have?

- How many downloads you have?

- What your audience engagement statistics look like?

- Where your reach goes, i.e. where is the podcast posted and how can people listen?

- Do you have an international audience?

- How do you promote your show?

- Will they have final approval before it airs? (always say no more on this later)

Some things to note as well for your own sanity. If someone doesn't respond to your e-mail, it likely means they are not interested. It is acceptable to send a follow up e-mail in the event that they just haven't had a moment to get to it. You may be familiar with the silence as an e-mail etiquette "*no*" and that's ok. Being interviewed is not everyone's cup of tea, or the request may have come at a bad time, or they might not feel it's a good fit for them. Don't take it personally, just move on. This is also why it is a good idea to have a list of a few guest options per episode.

Lastly, follow-up with your guest after the interview! Once your episode featuring your guest is live, send them a note to thank them for being on the podcast and include a link to the episode. Ask them to share it with their networks and post on social media should they feel so inclined. The biggest benefit to having someone on your show is the boost in audience. When they share with their network, you'll get free marketing and potentially a whole slew of new listeners.

Should your podcast require "*street*" interviews or interviews that happen on the fly, there are a couple of things to note. When interviewing someone on the street you have to state who you are and what you are doing verbally, it is recommended to do this on tape as well so you have a record that they agreed. Be sure they understand that you are recording them. It is illegal in the U.S. to record someone without their knowledge. Do let them know it is for a podcast that the public will hear. Once you have done all of that you'll need to have them sign a permissions waiver or release. This is something you can make yourself and it doesn't have to be anything too complicated. See Appendix I for an example. It's not always necessary to do this for someone you solicited over e-mail because you have the record of them agreeing. If you want to use a photo of them in marketing materials, however, you'll need to ask first and have them provide an approved image. If they do not have one, be sure and send them the one you plan on using so they can approve it ahead of time.

Panel Style Interviews

In the event that you would like to host a discussion between multiple people (and you have the equipment to support it), here are some tips.

Choose people who have a good rapport with each other. It is good to have multiple experts if you need that for your content, but the most important thing is that the conversation is listenable. How often has an academic paper been a page turner that keeps you glued to the text? Not usually the case. Remember that the panel needs to be approachable and have chemistry with one another. Also on that note, you want to make sure the group isn't *too* tight knit. You'll run into the inside joke issue I spoke about when choosing a co-host. The goal is to make the listener feel like they are at the table with the group, not on the outside being left out of the conversation.

As the host of the podcast, it's your job to moderate this conversation and group of guests. Be prepared with research and questions. Know when to guide the conversation and stay on topic, but also allow room for discovery and connection. Keep a mental note of who is talking as well, and encourage someone who isn't speaking enough to contribute by asking them a specific question only they can answer. Not everyone is comfortable in a group conversation. It is your job to make it so.

Most importantly, remember your role. If you are guiding a conversation between multiple guests, it's no longer about you. Help them shine. Contribute where it adds to the conversation, but not if it is going to pull from the flow and focus of the group.

Working with a Producer

An audio producer has a range of responsibilities, but for podcasting they are basically editing and mixing. Once you record your tape, you'd give it to a producer and they will edit out content, move things around in the story if it's an investigative journalism style podcast and they will put the finishing touches in. Adding music breaks, mixing the levels down or up, and smoothing out the audio to ensure it is a consistent volume for your listeners. Producing, in and of itself, is an artform based in technical know-how. Anyone can learn how to edit tape, but a true producer can finesse it and make your podcast sound professional and effortless. If you have the ability to work with a producer, you'll need to decide what type of producer meets your needs as a podcaster. There are many different levels out there that range from very basic editing to full on content production. I'm going to talk about the 3 main tiers of producers so you have a general idea of what to look for when working with a producer.

The most basic type of producer is usually called a producer but they are really more of a basic editor, like a copy editor for writing with fees ranging from $20-$75 per episode. They will only do what you ask them to. You'd provide clear instructions along the lines of *"cut question and answer at 11:37,"* or *"add music break at 20:17."* Their job is mainly to clean up the beginning and end of the podcast, cut whatever content you request (if you're lucky and you find someone willing to do this step), add music at the beginning and end as well as the intro and outro and then provide you with one file. They will not post your podcast for you or provide show notes. If you have the type of podcast that is done in one take, like a conversation between you and your co-host, or an interview only podcast with no more than 1 segment, using an editor is completely fine.

The mid-level is a Producer with fees typically landing around $120-$175 per episode. You would provide them with all of your content, segments, music etc. A Producer will piece it all together to match the format you have provided. For example:

> *Segment 1: Introduction of topic including monologuing*
>
> *Music Break: file name of music*
>
> *Segment 2: Interview with Bob Willis*
>
> *Music Break: file name*
>
> *Ad: file name*
>
> *Segment 3: poem*

They will do a little more than piecing the podcast together. They can clean up pauses, breaths, distorted audio or handling noise of a recorder. They will also mix and mastering of the audio for you so you have a nice clean file that sounds smooth and professional.

The highest level of producer is an Executive Producer. Executive Producers that are freelance or contract typically charge a day-rate because they aren't necessarily working on one episode at a time, but rather helping with the entire show. The industry standard is $500 a day for this kind of work. Working with an Executive Producer is much more of a partnership as they contribute to developing and maintaining the overall vision of the podcast. They do all of the things the mid-range Producer would in terms of organizing and mixing content, but their main role is to help you tell the best story. They will take the audio you give them and cut or rearrange content so it makes the most sense. They will also more than likely work with you to storyboard episodes so you know what kind of recordings you'll need to collect. Executive Producers are a lot like a publishing editor. They take what you've given them and make sense out of it. In addition, they will provide show notes and often post the podcast for you to all of the appropriate channels.

For a lot of podcasters, the production aspect is the most daunting. It is more costly to hire a producer, but using this information you can figure out what your needs actually are based on the type of podcast you've chosen to make. Of course, there is the option to produce the episodes yourself. I will cover those options in Chapter 6. It is not hard to learn audio production, but it is time consuming. If you want a high-quality sounding podcast and are anxious to get it off the ground, I'd recommend hiring someone. Just make sure it is someone you want to work with and you are respectful of what they have said they can deliver. Setting clear expectations on both party's end is always a good idea.

5. What Equipment Do You Need?

Getting set up with the correct tools to record and produce your podcast is extremely important. There is only so much a producer can do with bad tape. You'll need the right equipment to ensure you are getting the best recording possible, no matter the circumstance. The equipment requirements depend on the format of your podcast. If you are interviewing guests or monologuing in a home *"studio"* set up you'll need different outfits than if you are out in the world gathering content. You may also need a combination of both. We'll take a look at the grassroots approach and the sophisticated approach, both of which will be broken down into a studio set up vs. what you might need in the field. These recommendations are based on my personal experience and the equipment my clients and colleagues prefer. There are other options out there, I am just informing you of what the industry standards are.

The Grassroots Approach

The grassroots approach is for the thriftiest of podcasters. Podcasting expenses can add up once you take into account monthly hosting sites and production. Here I'll recommend equipment and software that will get the job done affordably without sacrificing quality.

If you are going to be out in the field as we say in radioland, as opposed to a controlled studio environment you are going to want a hand-held recording device. The *Zoom H4N Pro* or *Zoom H5* are great options for a quality device at a good price point. The great thing about Zoom is it has a very user-friendly manual and is easy to use right out of the box. It does not come with an SD card, however, so you'll need to purchase that separately in order to use the recorder. The *H4N Pro and H5* have two built in mics that can record in stereo and mono as well as an auto-limiter built in. This means that no matter how loud your audio peaks the *Zoom* automatically clips it so the sound isn't too heavily distorted. The screen clearly shows your levels and you

Zoom H4N Microphone

can set it up to record in the appropriate high-quality options for podcasting. It runs on four AA batteries and gets has decent battery life.

While the built-in mics on the *Zoom H4N Pro* and *H5* are good quality, it is recommended that you use external mics to reduce ambient noise when interviewing someone. The *Samson Q2U Handheld Dynamic USB Microphone Recording and Podcasting Pack* is the best bang for your buck. It is a great dynamic microphone that has the option to plug in to the *Zoom* through cables or through USB into your computer. So, you have the option to use it in your home to record voice over later if necessary. The pack comes with all the cords you need as well as a mic stand which is key when recording voice over or interviewing in a room and minimizes handling noise. If you are interviewing people use 2 mics, you do not want to be passing a microphone back and forth. Alternatively any dynamic microphone should do trick, I also like the *Shure SM58-LC Cardiod Dynamic Vocal Microphone.*

If you are going to be mono-casting and not in the field, I recommend the *Yeti Blue* mic. It connects to a computer via USB and has a great in studio sound. It does have the option to record two people, so two directions. The only downside to using it that way is that it is not a super sensitive mic so you'll both need to be very close to the mic for it to pick up your voices. 2 inches away max. This microphone is also a great option if you have a co-host who is not in the same place as you, you can both record into your computer separately. I will cover remote recording in chapter 6 with instructions on how to do that. If you are looking for something a little less expensive than the *Yeti Blue*, the *USB Microphone Kit by Maono* is also a good studio option for mono-casting.

When recording directly into your computer you'll need production software. *Audacity* is a great free option. It does everything you need for editing, but even if you don't want to produce your own pieces, it's the best option for recording. You'll be able to see the wave form as you go, monitor levels, and keep track of time.

Maono USB Microphone

I don't recommend using your phone to record audio, but if you are in a pinch or want that option get the *Zoom iQ6 microphone* attachment for iPhone. Shure also makes a good iOs condenser mic called the *Shure MV88*.

Shure MV88 iPhone Microphone

The last piece of equipment you need is over-the-ear headphones. I cannot stress this enough; you should never record audio of any kind without using headphones. Your ears do not hear the same thing as the recording device whether it is a field recorder or your computer. When recording you need to be hearing what the recorder is picking up, monitoring levels, etc. It is important to have over the ear headphones and not ear buds so you only hear what the recording is doing and no outside noise. Really any over the ear headphones will work, but if you want to be professional the *Sony MDR7506 Professional Large Diaphragm Headphone* is my recommendation. I like that they have a pouch they can fold into and an extra-long cord.

Sophisticated Approach

For those with more of a budget looking to make a very professional sounding podcast there are a lot of options out there. You can make a studio with a sound board and fancy microphones that hang from arms and have pop filters, but you can also up the field recorder game if you aren't going to exclusively be in a studio-like setting.

The best field recorder and industry standard, is a Tascam. They are a little more complicated to use than a *Zoom*, but they give you more control over the audio you are recording. The best one on the market is the *Tascam Linear PCM DR-100MKIII*. They are designed for audio engineers and audio designers, but easy to use once you know how. The *Tascam*, unlike the

Tascam DR40 Microphone

Zoom, has a rechargeable ion battery that charges with a USB port just like a smartphone. It does have a place for backup AA batteries in the back of the recorder, however. Another *Tascam* option that is a little easier to use than the *DR-100* and is still a great recorder is the *Tascam DR40X.*

For use with the *Tascam*, a condenser microphone – or shotgun mic – is best. You can use the microphone recommended above, but a shotgun mic gives you the most control. It is a directional microphone so it will only pick up sound that it is directly pointed at. It is ideal for interviews. Especially interviews in with loud background noise. The

Rode NTG2 Multi-Powered Condenser Shotgun Microphone is the preferred option of audio journalists. Alternatively another favorite condenser mic is the audio *technica at875r*. The main thing to know about any shotgun mic is that it runs off of something called phantom power. Any handheld recorder will have an option to switch to phantom power. On the Tascam, this means that the mic will be using the AA batteries to power it while the recorder itself still runs off of the rechargeable ion battery.

Audio Technica AT875R Microphone

For the sophisticated *"studio"* approach you'll need a mixer. Zoom recently released a sound board specifically for podcasters, the *LiveTrak L-8.* It looks and acts just like a radio station or DJ soundboard. Giving you lots of freedom to manage levels and host multiple mics for group interview situations. It also has the ability to plug a phone directly into it for remote recording. It's still best to use a program for that, which I will talk about in chapter 6, but in a pinch it's a great option to plug directly into the board.

If you're looking for something a little more low key than a full on sound board, I recommend the *Tascam US-2x2*. It's a USB Audio/MIDI interface that gives you control over mic levels and recording levels while being more portable and more discrete, but still professional. You can also use it with an iPad if you want to take your show on the road.

Even with the best mixer or sound board in the world, the quality of the sound really comes down to the microphone you are using. In the sophisticated home or office studio set up there is really only one choice. A condenser mic with a shock mount and pop screen. Typically, these hang from arms to keep hands free and remove any risk of the mic picking up noise from the table it is sitting on. The *Rode NT1-A* is a great option and has a package option that comes with the shock mount and pop screen so it's ready to go right out of the box. You just need a stand or hanging arm to mount the microphone on.

As far as software is concerned, the industry standard is *Pro Tools*. It's relatively affordable at under $30 a month and comes with cloud storage. You can record directly into it and then also use it as a

production software. Another great option is *Audition*, which is available through the Adobe suite. Audition is more user friendly and will absolutely get the job done at a high quality. If you are going to be working with a sound engineer or producer that is based in radio, you might want to stick with Pro Tools.

Sony MDR7506 Headphones

The same rule about headphones applies to the sophisticated approach as it does to the grassroots approach. You must always wear headphones when recording! If you want something fancier than the Sony headphones previously mentioned, *Sennheiser* is one of the best on the market. Any model by them really, but the *HD 380 Pro* is a great option because it keeps the audio as close to true as possible. You can use a wireless version as long as it has the option to connect an aux cord.

For other recommendations on handheld equipment refer to Transom's guide. It was published in 2012 but most of the equipment is still relevant and available. Unlike computers audio equipment doesn't shift in technology as often.

https://transom.org/2012/field-gear-good-better-best/

6. How to Set-Up the Podcast

Recording Your Podcast

I f you are using a field recorder to record your podcast, you'll need to consult the manual on how to operate it. In this section, I'm going to give you some tips, tricks, and rule of thumb for general things to know while recording. No matter what practice, practice, practice before you record yourself or a guest for final tape. Have other people listen to your tape. Listen to it with various media players, like iTunes or a production program like Audacity. Make sure you can hear yourself and if it's too quiet or too loud adjust for the next time.

Whether you are using a field recorder, mixer, or a mic that is plugged into your computer through the USB hub you're going to have to set and mind your levels. Do this before anything else. It is essential to set the levels at the beginning of an interview so you do not have to mess with them while you are engaged in conversation.

On a field recorder like the Zoom or Tascam the record button will flash red when you press it. You'll begin to see movement on the screen, the bars will fluctuate to the left and right as you speak. It is EXTREMELY IMPORTANT to note that when the light is *"flashing"* IT IS NOT RECORDING. This just means that the recorder is actively listening so you are able to set levels and hear what the recorder hears without having to record. This is helpful for us because it means we won't have to delete that 5 min of nonsense while we get the levels right. However, if you are still getting used to using the recorder, I recommend going ahead and recording as you take levels to ensure you don't forget to actually record. How do you actually record then? You press the record button AGAIN and when the light stays red, that means it is recording.

What are levels? Levels just refers to the loudness at which a thing or person is being recorded. It's not quite the same as volume. Volume gives you the ability to increase or decrease how loud something is after it has been mixed. The level you are recording at is essentially the baseline for that recording. It needs to be set correctly the first time. There are things that can be done in production to make the sound louder or quieter, but it is much better to get it right the first time. In Audio zero is very loud, almost anything above a zero will peak. Peaking essentially means that the sound the recorder is picking up is so loud it can't record it appropriately. It will sound blown out because the recorder has to clip it to protect itself.

Levels should always try to register between -12 and -6 decibels or db. On a field recorder the screen will show you the numbers as well as a rectangular meter that moves across the screen. On the computer you'll be able to see the actual wave form as you record in a program such as Audacity. The numbers will be on the far left at the edge of the track and a meter similar to the field recorder is in the top right-hand corner of the window. In either scenario you'll want to get yourself and your guest talking in order to set the levels correctly. You need to get them talking long enough to get a sense of how their voice might change. As a reminder from chapter 3, I usually ask my guest what they had for breakfast to get them talking so I can adjust the levels.

On the field recorder you'll either have a wheel to turn or + and – buttons to increase or decrease the levels. On a mixer there will be knobs associated with each microphone that can be turned to adjust the levels. On a soundboard there will be a sliding button with the numbers next to it in a range also associated with individual microphones.

Note: the higher the negative number, the louder the sound. So, -6 is louder than -12. Anything in that range is safe for good levels.

When setting levels, you need to make sure your headphone volume is not set too high or too low. This is tricky because you would think the levels on the recorder or computer would match the levels in your headphones, but they do not. If your headphone level is set too high, the levels you set on the recorder will likely be too low. The best thing to do is listen through the recorder or computer before your guest gets there. Just listen to the surrounding noises and maybe speak into the mic at a normal volume. Use that to set the baseline headphone volume. Once you've set your levels, if you are having trouble hearing someone and the numbers still read between -12 and -6, you can increase your headphone volume.

Typically, in a conversation things change as you and your guest get more comfortable around each other and the equipment. Someone might get animated and therefore, louder. If that happens when using the field recorder, simply control the levels by decreasing the mic distance from their mouth. Alternatively, if you are in a studio like setting, what generally happens is people pull away from the mic as they get more comfortable. They'll sit back in their chair and their levels will drop. Simply use a hand gesture to signal to them to move closer to the mic. If they aren't able to understand you, simply stop and tell them to move closer.

Before the Interview

Triple check your recording equipment. Make sure you are recording and levels are set correctly; be mindful that your headphone volume is not too high or too low as it will affect the levels in the overall recording.

Get interviewees on the mic. Get your guests right on top of the mic, no more than a couple inches away (4" max). People tend to shy away from the mic (particularly if seated at a table where they control their distance from the mic if there is a stand present). When they do, stop the interview and explain that they need to stay closer.

Introductions and names. Ask the interviewee to say and spell their name on tape. Then concisely introduce yourself AND your guests. Provide a short introduction synthesizing what the guest does, similar to a written bio. For example, *"I'm Amanda Mayo from WXPR Radio, and I'm here with Jenny Lee and John Dee of the band Random Band Name. Jenny sings and plays guitar, and John plays bass and keyboards."* Then head right into your questions.

Know your own verbal tics. Avoid *"um" "cool" "awesome,"* lip smacking etc.

Record room tone. If you are recording in the field or in a studio, BEFORE you leave the interview space (but after you thank the interviewee), record 30 seconds of room tone (the sound of the room without you talking). This will help your producer immensely in editing your tape.

During the Recording Process

Speak slowly and clearly. If you're the type of person that speaks a mile a minute. Remember to slow down and enunciate. Your listener can't see you; they don't have the visual cues of lip-reading or body language to help them follow your story.

Position your mouth 2-4 inches away from the microphone. No matter what type of microphone you are using, whether it be a field recorder, an XLR, or a shotgun mic, it is important to stay close to it so the mic is picking up you and not anything else. If it's too hard to eyeball 2-4inches, use your fingers. If you can fit 1-4 fingers in between your mouth and the mic, you're golden.

Mention names (of people, books, films, ideas, etc.) more than once. You know how *"As seen on TV"* ads say and show you the phone number around 5 times in 30 seconds? There's a reason for that, people aren't paying attention. We also use this trick during pledge drives in public radio because most people don't even hear the phone number or website until the 3rd time it's said. While I don't suggest hammering book titles and people's names into people's brains, it is a good idea to repeat information that is important. In addition to my examples above, podcasts are also consumed similarly to a book. Unlike a book, however, listeners can't go back and read or highlight an important thought they want to remember. It's your job to tell them what's important and remind them what you're talking about.

Listen intently and take notes while you listen. This isn't the first time I've mentioned this, but it deserves repeating. Until you get the hang of it, recording and participating in a conversation at the same time is difficult work. It takes intellectual labor to mind the levels, get used to equipment being in your face, and engage with your guest (or yourself in some cases). Remember to listen, *actually* listen, to the answers your interviewee is giving you and jot down something that catches your ear. This will help you formulate follow-up questions on the fly and keep the conversation flowing so it doesn't feel like a firing squad.

Keep your energy high. Again, you don't have the assistance of facial expressions and body language to help your listener feel engaged with your speaking voice. Even if you feel like you are a very high energy person in real life who speaks emphatically, more often than not that does not come across on the tape. If your voice sounds dead it will be torture for your audience and they will not listen. Think of it like pumping yourself up a couple notches. It's still you, just a really high energy you. As you practice this, you'll feel weird, but listen back to the tape and you'll see what I mean. It may seem like you were completely over the top, but it will just sound normal on the recording. One tried and true radio trick for keeping your energy up is to smile as you talk - listeners can hear it!

Don't be afraid of pregnant pauses. The best responses can come when an interviewee takes time to think of an answer or dwell in their thoughts. Another thing that bears repeating is to never speak over your guest or co-host. The easiest way to ensure this doesn't happen is to allow for someone to finish what they are saying and pause. They may think of something else they want to say and if you talk over them, it's lost forever in a muddled cloud of indiscernible audio.

Don't forget to share social handles and point listeners to show notes for more information. You've gotten through the interview and you're focused on closing it out so you might forget this detail. You can always add it in later in a voice over, but I find it's better to ask the guest to say their website and socials so it's on tape. This also ensures they are sharing the info they feel is most pertinent. Finish out by telling your listeners that the information from this episode will be available in the show notes on your website (or wherever you are publishing them).

Be thankful and appreciative to any guests. It should go without saying, but do thank them for coming on the show and show your gratitude. This also helps the interview come to a natural conclusion and can sometimes lead to further discussion that may not have happened otherwise.

Don't stop recording. When you've reached the end of your interview and you've done your sign off and such, it will be tempting to hit "*stop*." Don't do it. Just don't. 99% of the time you and your guest will still be chatting and they will say some gem of a quote. If you are not recording, it's lost forever. Wait until everyone has literally stopped talking and you are moving to walk them out of the studio or away from the recording equipment to stop recording. You can even wait until they are out of the building. It's not a big deal to trim off that dead silence or random conversation if it doesn't lead anywhere. It is a big deal to lose a great insight or quote.

Remote Recording

If you and your co-host don't live in the same place, or you need to record an interview with someone who is also not able to be in the room with you, you'll need to do a remote recording. Using something like Zoom or Skype is not recommended. The audio quality is awful and it will often crash because it doesn't have a stable internet connection. Please don't even consider using your phone on speaker.

Zoom, Google Video or call etc will not give you a file that is a high enough quality to be produced. It will also sound awful. Consider your audience. You need to do everything in your power to get people to listen, but also to *keep* people listening. If someone turns off your podcast halfway through, they likely will not tune in again. They most certainly won't sing your praises to their network, which is a large part of growing your listener-base. They'll simply forget you exist. Since podcasting has taken off, there are many remote recording options out there! I implore you, use one of these services. Here are a couple affordable apps that I recommend and know work great.

Zencastr lets you record 8 hours for free each month with up to 2 guests. At the free level you receive an Mp3 of the recording. The paid version is $20 a month and gets you a WAV file, unlimited recording time, and unlimited storage for your recordings. In the paid version it even gives you the option to use a *"mixing board"* program so you can insert your intros, outros, and music, if you are not using a producer and are able to get your interview done in one take. In addition you'll also have access to automated post production of your files that means you'll essentially have a finished podcast at the end of the call. Zencastr uses voice over IP (VOIP), so while it is going through the internet it is a much more secure line. This significantly decreases the chances of freezing or audio dropping out due to a poor internet connection. It also gives you a link to share with your guests. There is nothing to download to configure on their end. They simply click the link and voila you are connected!

Ringer is another great affordable service out there right now. It does a lot of the same things Like Zencastr they also send a special link to your guest. There are two plans on Ringr, basic at $7.99 a month and premium at $18.99 a month, although you can try it free for 30 days.

The basic plan provides you with a mono track, unlimited call recordings, unlimited storage, and an Mp3 of your file. The mono track means all voices are recorded on the same track, which is not ideal, but is also not the end of the world. The premium plan gives you split tracks (each voice in a separate file), WAV files, unlimited storage, and conference calling. The conference calling option is great if you need to speak with more than 2 people at a time, like in a panel style interview podcast. One of the other really cool things about Ringr is it gives your guests the option to use their cell phone to make the call, rather than just the computer option. This is great for people who don't want to talk at their computer with no video. If your guests are going to use this feature, just make sure you let them know they need to be in a quiet place and not moving around a ton. While the quality is still great, nothing can be done with outside noise if they are walking around outside on a busy street with sirens and honking cars.

You may be wondering how remote recording works in terms of files and editing. I mentioned split track and mono tracks above. Let me break that down a little more. A split track means each person is recorded on their own track. A split track is preferred as it gives you or your producer freedom to edit each person individually. A mono track means everyone speaking is recorded on one track. The downside to a mono tracks is it gives you less flexibility in post-production. Let's say while you are talking and your guest is silent, they bang the table or are breathing into their microphone. Those noises are recorded through their microphone, but not picked up on yours. The dead air and noises can be cut out of their track so it doesn't hinder the listeners experience giving you a much more professional cut. If the track is in mono and there are noises like that, they can't be cut unless it happens during a pause when no one is talking. It is very difficult to remove those types of noises when you can't isolate it, or if someone is talking when they happen.

Because there are so many great options available to podcasters for remote recording, there really is no excuse for bad tape. It also opens up a lot of doors for you to be able to interview whoever you want no matter where they are. Paris? No problem. 2 time zones over? Yep. Australia or Japan? You got it. Talk to your heroes without spending thousands of dollars on a plane ticket!

Editing / Post-Production

Since we already covered the roles of a producer in Chapter 4, this section will speak to the DIY approach. I'll talk about how to edit for content to enhance your story and give you some options for production programs you can use.

Editing for content is important as it helps tighten up the conversation and the story. I will note that ethically you should not edit to change the meaning behind what someone is saying. You are editing to make things clearer. Here's an example through text:

Host: *So when would you say you felt the spark of an idea for your project?*

Guest: *uh......well...it was...I'd say...sometime in 2013...no wait, 2014 was when the idea really started to formulate.*

As a producer, the way I would edit the guest's response is like this:

[Uh......well...it was]...I'd say... [sometime in 2013...no wait,] 2014 was when the idea really started to formulate.

The brackets denote what I would take out, so the guest's answer would then be:

I'd say 2014 was when the idea really started to formulate.

See how much cleaner that is? You're also going to want to take out long pauses, lip smacking, and any kind of pops or handling noise you might get from the recorder.

When you are making cuts, you want it to sound natural and still like a conversation. Generally, it is easy to see where you might like to make a cut in an audio program because you can actually see the audio in wave form. See Fig 6. Trust your ears more than your eyes here. You always want to edit on the breath if there is one. This means leaving space between the words that sounds natural. For example, if someone breathes out or in before speaking a word keep that moment and cut just before it. Sometimes I close my eyes to retrain my brain to listen for that natural pause rather than just watching it scroll on by in the waveform. If you are up against a tight waveform because the person is not taking pauses, or their words blend together you can cut where the phrase you want to use starts, and insert a breath-long excerpt from the room noise you collected when recording.

A similar rule of thumb applies to music. You always want to fade your music in and out of each segment. The fades should also start and end as someone is talking. This makes it a smooth transition for your listener's ears. They'll start to hear the music as the person speaking is finishing their thought, indicating that a break is coming and the next segment will follow. 8-10 seconds is a good length of fade, making it not too long and not abrupt. You also want to apply a similar technique to cutting on the breath with music. Listen for when it makes sense to start and stop the music. For example, if you are using music that has a natural build and crescendo and then evens back out, you don't want to cut the music in the middle of a crescendo. You want to find where that transition in the music takes place and cut it there. Similarly, if you are using a song that has a singer in it, don't cut the music in the middle of a verse.

Onto **software** options. The best free audio editing software out there is *Audacity*. This software is a real professional audio production program and it's relatively easy to use. There are plenty of tutorials out there on YouTube to get yourself familiarized with it. It works with Macs, Windows, and Linux. You can also record directly into it, which I recommend if you are going with the studio style set up. Audacity is great if you want to have a lot of control over your own editing process. It's also just a good idea to have it on your computer regardless of how you decide to edit your podcast. The other automated production apps I'm going to recommend are limited in what they can do. It's a good idea to familiarize yourself with Audacity in the event that you need to make a specific type of edit that you can't in the other programs.

Alitu is a new fully automated production assistant. It bills itself as being a sort of one-stop-shop for podcasters, but you can use whatever parts of it suit your needs. The main concept behind it is that you can record your podcast into it, edit it, and publish it to your host while also taking care of posting to all major distributors. *Alitu* is a good editing solution. The control you have over the files is minimal, but that's not necessarily bad depending on your format. *Alitu* automatically converts and cleans up your files, snaps together your recordings, adds your music fades, and publishes to your host. There are customized tools to help you take out mistakes and pauses. It will also help you create music and create ads or segments with music beds. They are continuing to add features to what the program can do as well. The cost is $28 a month, which is about the same for *ProTools* or *Adobe Audition*. For someone who doesn't necessarily want to learn full on audio production, but still wants a professional sounding podcast, this is a great option.

Anchor is also touted as an all-in-one option. You can record, edit, host, publish, and even monetize your podcast through this app. As an editor the options are even more minimal and you can only edit on a phone or iPad. They are working on an online desktop version, but a release date has yet to be announced. There are lots of options for transition music and sound effects to help break up your segments and make it sound professional. It also renders it with a mixed file in the end to give it that studio quality sound. Anchor is one of, and possibly the only truly free hosting service out there. It boasts unlimited storage and uploads and will also publish to all major distributors once you post your episode. For the monetization component they identify and match your show with brands that can advertise on your podcast. You're given a script by the advertiser and you record it to ensure it stays on brand. There is also a listener support button added to your podcast page, so listeners can send you monthly donations to help keep the show going if they choose. Additionally, *Anchor* now provides a remote recording option. Your guest would need to install the app but they are able to engage in a call with you that records directly into *Anchor.* I personally cannot vouch for the quality of an Anchor remote recording as I have not heard one.

If you are really serious and want to become an audio producer alongside your podcasting duties, there is a decent amount of audio software available. The industry standard for radio and most podcasters working in radio is *Pro Tools*. Many producers prefer *Audition* because its interface is a little more user friendly. It is less complicated and buggy than Pro Tools. Other programs producers like are *Hindenberg* and *Reaper*. Hiring a producer is easy. There are lots of production companies out there that can assist you with all aspects of your podcast. This book gives you the tools to do most things on your own. You should be able to use your format to give clear instructions to a producer. So, if you need to hire someone to edit your audio, *Upwork* is a great place to find producers of all levels.

Audio production is not particularly hard to learn, but it is extremely tedious and time consuming. There is a little bit of instinct needed to be a good producer, but basic editing skills can certainly be learned. Just consider where your time is best spent and if it is realistic for you to teach yourself audio production vs using a producer or *Alitu* and *Anchor*. I always say work smarter, not harder! If it's smarter for you to use an automated editing app or hire a producer, then do it. It'll sound great and save you time!

A Note about Show Notes

All podcasts have show notes, as they should because what if you missed the name of that really cool book the host and their guest just spend 40 minutes talking about and you can't find it no matter how many times you rewind? The worst. Show notes are basically just notes about your show, but really notes about your episode. They should be posted with every episode and they live on your podcast website. Notes are not posted in the description field on your host or Apple podcasts, but rather in the longer description box when you post the episode to your website.

Example from NYTimes, The Daily:

On today's episode:

- Amy Chozick, a writer at large for The New York Times covering the personalities and power struggles in business, politics and media.

Background reading:

- *Adam Neumann had an inexplicably persuasive charisma and a taste for risk. Then he found a kindred spirit with an open checkbook.*

- WeWork is preparing to eliminate at least 4,000 employees, cutting nearly a third of its work force in an effort to staunch further financial losses.

- Tune in, and tell us what you think. Email us at thedaily@nytimes.com. Follow Michael Barbaro on Twitter: @mikiebarb. And if you're interested in advertising with "The Daily," write to us at thedaily-ads@nytimes.com.

There are a few ways to tackle show notes and there is a pretty broad spectrum of what you can include. Here are the things that should always be included:

- Short episode summary (you can re-use your apple podcast episode description).

- Links to your website and social media platforms.

- Links to your guest's (if you are doing an interview) website and social media platforms.

- A note and link to any important books, music, people, news etc. that you mention in the podcast.

In addition to those more basic show notes, you can really get expansive on what you include. Some podcasts, particularly news outlets, like to include a full transcript of the episode. This is particularly handy if your audience might need to be able to read the information in your podcast vs listening to the whole thing. Transcripts are really time consuming, even with paid software that helps to automatically translate the audio to text.

Another more in-depth version of show notes that is not quite as time consuming as transcripts, but still really helpful are time stamped quotes. These are a great thing to include because it helps a listener know what is truly covered in an episode so they can make the decision to tune in or not. It's also helpful for those social media shares because it gives your audience something they can copy and paste to their own social networks. Also helpful for those who might need to cite your podcast in something else whether it's another podcast, press, or the media. Providing these quotes and where to find them, ensures you're not misquoted.

A Couple Examples:

3:03 Segment 1: Amanda speaks with Jane Jack about her decision to include this piece at the Art Institute.

15:17: Segment 2: We head to the Art Institute to get their take on public engagement with Jane Jack's piece.

Or

5:47: Jane Jack describes her piece, The End of Everything, "The work is really about our relationship to climate change and how I can get the viewer to experience the extreme emotional loss that will come with the death of our ecosystem.

Sometimes producers will write and post the show notes for you, be sure to ask if this is included in their fee. Usually it's good for the producer to at least write the show notes because they are the ones spending so much time with the episode, they know where things are and what to include etc. It really depends on the level of producer you are working with. Obviously, if you are producing your own episodes writing and posting show notes falls to you.

An additional piece of information to include in show notes is a link to subscribe to your newsletter, if you have one. Typically, whoever you host your newsletter through (mailchimp, constant contact, etc.) will have an embedded code or a link that you are able to copy and paste. That link will prompt whoever clicks on it to subscribe to your newsletter by providing their email. They are then automatically added to your mailing list in your newsletter host. Always a good idea to include this link in your show notes and any communications related to your podcast over email or on a website.

The main take away is that you should include show notes that are helpful to your listener and give an idea of the specific things that are included in your episode. Based on listener feedback, you can tweak these notes to include more of what they'd like more information on, etc. As a starting point, provide what you think the most important ideas and resources are in each episode.

Music Licensing

As previously mentioned, podcasting is currently the Wild West of media. They are not monitored by any overarching government regulators. I will talk about FCC rules and provide a resource for legal info for podcasting in general in the next chapter. I do want to touch on music licensing here. As you may know, art is subject to copyright. Music falls under that category. Musicians are paid a royalty every time their music is played where it can be consumed by public ears. Streaming is a bit different, but I'm not going to get into that here. If you are curious you can research that on your own. Radio stations apply for, are given, and pay for a broadcast license. This allows them to play music on the air, but it is also their duty to report the music they have played so the almighty people behind the music regulating curtain can pay out royalties to the artists. That is how a radio station is able to play copyright music.

Just like any other type of art, you can't just take it and use it in something you've made. Music licenses are not new – advertisers, television, online videos, movies, etc. all have to pay for the use of someone's song. Podcasting is no different, however, the fees and terms of license use are still changing and have not normalized as of yet. You'll need royalty-free music, since there isn't a way to track song play amounts like at a radio station.

The safest thing to do is to create your own music for your podcast, because it is created for this explicit purpose you own the rights to the music. You can also pay a musician to make theme music for you. Just be sure to have a contract indicating who owns the rights to the song and that you are paying one time for continuous use.

If you are not musically savvy, however, and you want to have music in your podcast (which you should) there are many great options for music out there. Luckily, there are tons of music sites that you can purchase tracks from. When you purchase from these sites you are purchasing the license and the ability to legally use the music you have bought. Each site has different levels of licenses. Almost all of them hinge on how many listeners you have, how many downloads, and whether or not your podcast is a commercial podcast.

There is something called a Creative Commons (CC) license. Creatives have submitted their work to Creative Commons (creativecommons.org) for free use. Just be wary, you have to follow the license instructions to a "*T.*" Typically that just means proper attribution and noting the license number, but some have additional instructions. The other issue, is it's entirely possible that someone will remove the piece you have chosen to use from Creative Commons later on and then all of your past episodes will be in breach of license. If that happens, you'll have to contact the person directly to purchase a license from them.

Sites like Audio Jungle and Jamendo have a massive selection and clear music licenses. You can apply all sorts of filters from mood, to genre, style, vocals vs no vocals, etc. to find the perfect jam for your podcast. The upside is that most of the music found on these sites is written with the intention of having vocal tracks laid over it. It is easy to cut and use as a music bed without being distracting. If you are going to be using different songs or sound effects, you can purchase a subscription to some sites which you pay a monthly fee to use and that gains you access to an ongoing license. Otherwise you have to purchase individual licenses for each song or sound effect you want to use.

Unfortunately, because the landscape is ever changing with podcasting, there is no comprehensive guide to music licenses. There is also no standard fee across the board. Be diligent in purchasing and maintaining whatever music license you go with to ensure you don't run into legal troubles. Essentially, just do your research before you mix in any music.

Preventing Problems

How can you set yourself up for success to ensure your recordings are the best quality they can be? Make a list of every possible thing that can go wrong and then make sure it doesn't. If only it were that simple! I have a checklist that I go through before each interview or voice over to ensure I've got everything I need in proper working order. I also have back-up plans for the rare event that trouble shooting doesn't resolve my issue. Here are some checklists to help you stay prepared:

Equipment:

- ☐ Field recorder charged + fresh back up batteries in case.
- ☐ Microphone cheat sheet.
  - I include a small cheat sheet with the settings for using an XLR and the built-in mics in my kit to help me troubleshoot if something isn't working in the moment.

- [ ] XLR Mics x 2.

- [ ] XLR cable(s).

- [ ] Back-up mic for phone.

- [ ] Headphones.

- [ ] Solid red means record, flashing red means caution you're not recording!

- [ ] Check headphone volume.

  - make sure it's not too high or too long as it will affect your levels.

- [ ] Play recording back.

  - As soon as you've stopped recording, press play to make sure it recorded.

Interview Prep:

- [ ] Notes or outline transferred to phone.

  - even if I am using a paper notebook, I still transfer the outline or questions to my phone's note section in the event that I forget my notebook or something happens to it.

- [ ] Opening and closing statement

Software and File Saving:

- [ ] Take file off recorder.

- [ ] Save file to DropBox.

  - I always directly save either a computer recorded or field recorded file to DropBox. You can use some sort of cloud* but be extra diligent about this. If you lose that file, you've lost your podcast.

☐ Take notes.

- shortly after you finish your interview or monologuing, take notes while it's fresh in your mind. You're not gonna want to listen to 40 minutes of tape 3 weeks later. Trust me.

*a note about Google Drive: anything that is kept on Google Drive or Google Docs is actually property of Google. In most cases this doesn't matter, but recordings are sensitive because they are a record of what someone has said. Keep this in mind if you are planning on using Google Drive to store or share files.

7. How to Launch Your Podcast Successfully

The Essentials

You've done all the work; you've got your great podcast in the can ready to be released into the world. What else do you need to do to get it out there? For starters, if you haven't thought of one already, you need a **title**! You need to love your title because it is going to be everywhere. Here are some helpful tips for picking the right title.

Title

Make it catchy. Your title should be representative of your podcast and you. It should be specific and evocative.

Keep it short. You need to consider clipping and how the title shows up in an internet search. Make sure it's not going to get shortened in apple podcasts, or other distribution sites. Here are some interesting statistics from Pacific Content[4]:

- Half of all podcast titles are between 14 and 29 characters.

---

[4] https://blog.pacific-content.com/the-art-and-science-of-naming-your-podcast-58399308066a

- The most popular title length is 16 characters.

- The mean average show title is 23.9 characters.

- The median show title is 20 characters.

Don't include *"podcast"* in your title. Just don't. People will know it's a podcast and any SEO search for your title followed by the word podcast will deliver your podcast results. Because your podcast is being posted on podcast sites, distribution platforms, apple podcasts etc., it already has that meta tag imbedded in its data. No need to include the type of media (podcast) in your title. Think about it like this, the Gmail app is not called *"Gmail app."*

Avoid clever spelling. Podcasts largely travel by word of mouth, so don't name it something with a play on spelling or pronunciation. That makes it incredibly difficult to search.

Cover your bases. Google the title you've chosen, make sure there aren't any other websites, blogs, books, and heaven forbid – podcasts with your title! It would also be a good idea to check trademarked names to be sure there isn't an active trademark out there on your name. If you don't do these things, you risk receiving a cease and desist order as well as just confusing your potential audience. Your title is you, it's your brand, it also happens to be your podcast!

Be sure to also check social media handles. It's not as big of a deal as the things listed above because you can differentiate a little more on social media, but check anyway to make sure it's not going to be impossible to find you.

Buy your domain name. Even if you already have a website or you choose to build a website through your hosting service, it's a good idea to purchase the title of your show as a domain name. This ensures that you own it and no one else can snatch it up. They are so inexpensive to purchase so I recommend doing this. If your podcast takes off and you are able to build it into a full on brand you'll regret not having done this from the start.

Apple ID. This is related to title, but also just a good rule of thumb. It is recommended that you create a new Apple ID for your podcast. This makes it easier to track things and gives you more solidarity with your brand. Just make sure it's tied to an e-mail you use frequently and you also have a password you will always remember for it. If you get locked out of the email associated with your podcast's Apple ID you're out of luck. Nothing can be done. Pertinent communications regarding your standing in apple podcasts will be communicated to you through that ID and email.

Images

Another thing that is required of your podcast is an image. This is the image that will post to your show's "*page.*" It will show up as a thumbnail in searches on distribution sites, apple podcast, Spotify, podcast apps etc. Apple podcasts set the standard on what's required in terms of size and quality, which bleeds over to all other hosts and distributors, apps, and Spotify. The image needs to be square and contain original content. If you are going to use a photograph, make sure it is yours or a stock photo you have the right to use. Your photo should be clearly designed so it can be viewed easily as a thumbnail. It's a good idea to include your title in the design of the image, just make sure it is still readable.

Minimum size: 1400 x 1400 pixels.

Maximum size: 3000 x 3000 pixels.

Use RGB color space.

File must be under 500kb.

JPEG, JPG, or PNG files are acceptable *(if you are using PNG, don't have it set to transparency, it will be blurry in the Apple podcast store).*

You also have the option to make a new image for each episode. Same rules apply in terms of size and design. You can make it slightly different than your overall show image. Use it as a way to further solidify your brand image. Keep it in a similar vein by using the same design but choosing a different color scheme, or make it the same color scheme with a different design overall. It's not necessary to have one for each episode, you can just use your show image, but this is an option if you'd like to differentiate your episodes. Where it's helpful to have different images is for scrolling purposes. When folks are scrolling through your episodes in an app, it'll differentiate each episode.

A great free tool online is *Canva*. It's a design website that gives you all sorts of templates and marketing tools. You can design your show image in there and then use all their other great templates for social media posts, business cards, postcards etc. anything to solidify your podcast brand.

Descriptions

Next up is descriptions. You're going to need a few different descriptions of varying lengths.

The main one is the overall description that lives on your show page, which is on your website, but also on apple podcasts which feeds into the other distribution sites. The Apple podcast search results teaser cuts off the description after 50 words adding *"see more..."* in order to view the whole description. You're going to want to make sure your first 50 words are really engaging. You can use your elevator pitch to start off. In total it shouldn't be more than 200 words. The main goal of this description is to say what the podcast is, and what people can expect to hear in general. This is the main reason people will listen to your show, it is your first point of contact to someone just randomly searching for a podcast to listen to. Make sure your description addresses what's in it for them.

As an example let's look at WJCT's *Odd Ball*. I love their descriptions. The shorter description that shows up in apple podcasts is:

Odd Ball is a story about a UFO investigation, a mansion in the woods and how one shiny object sent a Jacksonville, Florida family into hiding. Each week host Lindsey Kilbride dives deeper into the 1974 mystery of the "Betz sphere."

Clocking in at 41 words, it's the perfect length for the general description page in all podcast platforms.

A longer description should be written for your own website. This one can go more into who you are, why you are doing this podcast, what you hope to put out there. Also include similar things to the apple general description to keep things consistent. Use it as a space to expand on what your podcast is for those who may be seeking more information. Again, *Odd Ball* has a great longer description on their website:

In 1974 Gerri Betz and her son Terry found a metal sphere on their property on Jacksonville's Fort George Island.

Not long after, witnesses say the ball started vibrating and seemingly rolling with its own volition. The family poodle would whimper and cover its ears near the ball. That's when the Navy and nationally-renowned UFO scientists took an interest in investigating the ball. Gerri was excited by the attention at first. She was known to those around her as smart and sharp, starting a lucrative trucking business on her own and running for a state House seat. But then people started showing up at her door wanting to see the ball and pay for it.

Today she doesn't speak of the ball. Odd Ball *aims to figure out what the ball could have been, who has it and if there's any way Gerri will finally talk.*

This description is great because it tells the premise of the podcast, what the podcast is going to do and tell you, all while leaving a little mystery as to pique your interest.

You absolutely need a tag line or two. These will go on any social media handles you have. In the "*bio*" section on Instagram and twitter and the "*about*" section on Facebook. The tagline also needs to be short and catchy. I know, shocking! Keep it simple and memorable. As a writer, podcaster, and coach my tagline is "*Tell me your story, I'll tell the world!*" It's not complicated or fluffy, but it works for what I need.

It identifies me as a storyteller in any form a story can be told whether that be podcasting or writing. People remember it based on how I've been introduced to them, if they know me as a podcaster, they remember that. If they know me as a writer, they remember it equally as well. When a project comes up, they'll remember my tagline and my name because it's associated with it. That's what you want – people to remember.

Social Media

The last step in setting up your essentials is social media. If you have an enormous online following (or even a small one) it may feel daunting or counterintuitive to set up a separate account for your podcast. You need to do this. Your podcast has its own host, website, and show page, it also needs to have its own Twitter, Facebook, Instagram, and whatever else you want to use. If you have a million followers on your Instagram, that's great! You can use your personal page to direct people to your show.

Why is it important to have separate social media accounts for your podcast? Because the internet is how communication travels. Through tagging accounts, hashtags, mentions, (at)ing someone the world can see and easily find your podcast. If someone listens to an episode and loves it, they are going to blast it out there with your account linked to their post. Then people can click on the account and be brought right to your virtual doorstep. They can follow you so they don't forget to tune in when you drop an episode, or so they don't forget that they meant to listen to you. Instagram is the new business card and your podcast is your new business.

Hosting and Distribution

All podcasts need a host. Your host is what provides you with your RSS feed, which is how your podcast is distributed into the world. Hosts allow you to upload and store your podcast. In case you don't know what an RSS feed is, it's a way for people to receive updates on web-based content. You know that *"subscribe"* button you've probably clicked thousands of times in your lifetime? That's an RSS feed. When you subscribe, it gives the RSS feed permission to let you know when a new podcast, or blog post is live and ready for you to consume. It automatically shows up in your podcast player with a new episode.

Because of the need for digital storage space and distribution help, podcast hosting sites cost money. There are tons of options out there, but I will talk about a few recommendations.

There are currently only two truly free hosting services. One I've already talked about in Chapter 6 because it is also a production tool – *Anchor*. Anchor will allow you unlimited uploads and storage for free. Don't ask how, I have no idea. The other is *Squarespace*. There is a special plug-in for Squarespace websites that allows you to get an RSS feed and upload podcasts through them. The instructions are easy to find on the internet, but essentially you make a blog page and insert the plug in that way.

Libsyn is the industry standard for podcast hosting. They have been around the longest and are compatible with pretty much everything. The least expensive membership is $5, but that only gives you 50mb of upload storage per month, which is almost nothing. That could potentially be a 10-12 min podcast, but only one. The next level is $15 a month, then $20, and finally $40. With each level your upload and storage space increases. Your audience analytics also increase with each level. This basically means you get more detailed insights into your listeners, which is always helpful for marketing and tightening up your work. Libsyn provides you with players which can be embedded into an outside website if you like. Their plug-ins are compatible with almost all the major website hosting services (WordPress, Wix etc.) A membership also comes with a separate podcast website if you want to use theirs. The other benefit to being part of the Libsyn community is free advertisement. They have their own platform for helping people find podcasts. If you host with them then you are automatically fed into that feed and if you get popular enough they will include you in their top podcast picks. Another great perk of using Libsyn is your access to On Publish, which is an all-in-one social media posting program. You can basically write and schedule one social media post and On Publish will post it on all of your accounts, effectively saving you from having to tailor 5 different posts to 5 different social media accounts. An added bonus in my opinion. On Publish is its own program so if you like that idea, but don't want to use Libsyn as your host you can sign up for On Publish on your own.

A newer hosting site that has gained a lot of popularity among first time podcasters is *Simplecast*. There are 3 levels of monthly subscription options on this hosting service. The first is $15, the second is $35, and the last is $85. They all come with unlimited storage and uploads. The main differences between the levels is how many team members you can grant access to managing the podcast, customizations on embedded media players, and audience insights. You still get great analytics delivered to you at every level, but they have a new more specialized insight option that exists in the middle and higher end membership. Like Libsyn, it allows you to distribute to all major podcast distributors and provides you with your own website.

Other popular sites are **Blubrry, Buzzsprout**, and **Captivate** (particularly centered on audience growth).

Once you choose a host it's a good idea to stick with them, but in the event that you decide to change hosts later on, it's not the end of the world. Most hosting sites are set up to transfer your library with your RSS feed to your new host with minimal disruption to your listeners. There's always the chance that it won't go smoothly though, so be sure and give your hosting decision a critical eye.

Once you have your RSS feed through a host and some sort of audio content to post, either an episode or a trailer, you can submit your podcast to apple podcasts. It is a good idea to do this at least 2 weeks before you launch your podcast. Apple can take up to 10 days to approve and post your podcast. As previously mentioned, create a separate Apple ID for your podcast that is connected to the email you will be using for all podcast communication. Submitting to Apple Podcast is really quite simple now, much easier than it used to be with iTunes (R.I.P.) See *Essentials* section for image and description requirements. The steps to submit are simple and can be found online if you can't figure it out through the Apple store. Start by googling *"podcast connect"* and log in with your podcast Apple ID. You'll receive an email once it has been approved and is posted.

With your RSS feed all set up and your podcast posted in Apple podcasts, you can now start setting up your distribution. Most hosts distribute your podcast to all major platforms automatically but there are some you need to submit your RSS feed to on your own. The major podcast platforms are:

- Apple Podcasts
- Google Podcasts
- Stitcher
- Spotify
- Overcast
- Pocket Cast

Spotify and Stitcher need to be submitted to individually. Luckily, it's just like Apple in that you only have to submit and get your RSS feed approved once. When that is complete your RSS feed is connected to the platforms and will automatically post new episodes when you post them in your host.

Launch Strategy

How do you launch your podcast successfully? Well, it's a good idea to have some strategy behind releasing your podcast. Unfortunately, posting it and hoping for the best is not going to get you many listeners.

Solidify Your Posting Schedule (AND STICK TO IT!)

First of all, you are going to want to decide on your posting schedule. I've talked about consistency being important, but I'd like to stress it again here. Once your podcast is established and you have an audience, your listeners are going to be depending on that release day. This is the first duck to get in a row, pick a day of the week for your podcast to air and then stick to it!

Make a Trailer

In order to get your RSS feed going you need content to post. Additionally, Apple podcasts can take up to 10 days to approve a new podcast, and Spotify takes a few days as well. Having a trailer to release not only helps you promote your new podcast, but it alleviates the issue of getting your podcast out on the correct day the first time. The trailer can be released anytime and then when it's time to post your first episode it can adhere to your posting schedule to set the precedent for when listeners can expect to hear new episodes. It's generally a good idea to release to trailer a month ahead of time, this will help you generate buzz and because it's linked to your RSS feed through your host, listeners can "*subscribe*" as soon as they hear about it. That way, when your first episode is live, it's already in their podcast listening queue.

A podcast trailer is a not that long, 90 seconds to 3 min tops. A good "*coming soon*" trailer, which is what you'll need for launching is engaging and informative.

- Showcase what you'll be delivering with each episode of your podcast.

- Cover the who, what, why, when, and where.

- Include short clips from upcoming episodes.

- Provide some highlights on who will be on your podcast or what topics you'll be diving into.

- Include where people can find more information and subscribe (i.e. website, social handles, etc).

Remember that the trailer lives on well into your podcast episodes. Apple will often pin the trailer to the top of the feed in your podcast feed because they know it is a great way to introduce listeners to your show. Make something that really makes your audience want to listen!

Digital Footprint

Make sure your digital footprint is ready to go. Ensure your podcast website is how you want it, or if you are integrating it into your own website check to make sure that is all running smoothly.

- Include a photo of yourself and a bio.

- Have an about page on your website that holds your longer description about the podcast.

- Get your social media handles set up and branded.

- If you are doing a newsletter, create a template and get your mailing list contacts added.

- Set-up an email list. Always be collecting emails from people who want to hear about what you're up to and store those away. Add people from your communities and networks so when you have news to share or something to promote, the list is already ready to go!

This way you are ready to announce your first episode on release day and you can shout about your podcast from the roof tops with your trailer to generate some interest.

Build Community

Online communities have become an efficient and effective way to network. Join Facebook groups that are in line with your podcast content and who you are as a person. Be sure to introduce yourself and what you're working on to drum up some support. When release day rolls around make special posts for each group to share the link to your first episode. This is a great way to start collecting listeners.

Building a small audience pre-launch is critical to thriving. The best-case scenario is getting features in Apple Podcast's **"New and Noteworthy"** podcasts. This gets you featured for 8 weeks on the landing page of Apple Podcasts. Unfortunately Apple keeps their algorithms close to the vest. There's no real way to quantify how they choose what makes it onto a chart or into the *"New and Noteworthy"* section of Apple podcasts. We do know there are a few key factors that play into the algorithm, however. Reviews, downloads, ratings, and listens are the major ones. Since you won't have an audience built up when you launch it's imperative that you reach out to your community and networks ahead of time. Implore them to rate your podcast, leave reviews, download and subscribe. The more 5 star ratings and reviews you have the higher your chances are of being featured in that coveted *"New and Noteworthy"* section.

Hold a Launch Event

Use the options listed above to help generate buzz online, but you should also hold a launch event. It should be something creative and hopefully in line with what your podcast is about.

For example: if your podcast is about cycling – hold a party at a local brewery and offer a drink ticket to anyone who rides their bike there.

Or

Hold a community bike ride that ends at a venue for the launch party and partner with the venue to provide some cool swag as incentive. Hold a raffle where people have to "subscribe" to your podcast to get a raffle ticket.

Even though it's not guaranteed, launching your podcast this way will help you to organically grow a listener base. Whatever event you decide to do to launch your podcast, be sure it targets your audience and is on brand with what they'd like to attend.

Launch with 3 Episodes

Have more than one episode ready to go. Have at least 2, preferably 3, episodes posted on launch day. This will increase your chances of getting into that *"new and noteworthy"* section because listeners have the option to listen to more than one podcast increasing your listens and downloads. The other main reason for posting more than one episode is so your listener can really get an idea of what your podcast is about.

Your first episode should stick to your format, but be more introductory. It will act as a springboard into who you are, why you are doing the podcast and what people can expect to hear. Your second episode is then an actual episode of the podcast and what it will sound like moving forward. This gives your audience a chance to get to know you and then learn what to expect from your podcast by listening to more than one episode.

Plus, people love to binge. That act is not exclusive to Netflix. Be sure you have a couple other episodes waiting in the wings to help you stay on track with your posting schedule as well. Meaning you'll need to have 5 episodes finished and ready, 3 of which you will post on launch day. The other 2 will stay in the can. This will give you time to effectively market your next episodes after the launch without having to scramble to get them produced. It also builds in some cushion for your production schedule so you can stay true to your posting schedule.

Keep it Up

Don't stop! Once launch day passes, don't hang up your hat and get back to the grind. Keep the buzz going. Piggy back on friends or listeners who are sharing your podcast on social media, comment, like, re-post etc. Send reminder e-mails to your contacts asking them to check out your new podcast if they haven't already. Let people know how it's going. Folks love a concrete number, tell them you are so grateful to hit 495 subscribers, and put a call to action out there!

"Can we hit 525 by the end of today? Help me by sharing this link!"

Keep building your community!

Legal Considerations

If you get to the point where you want to be able to submit your podcast to a radio station for on-air broadcast, you're going to have to be able to deliver an FCC approved show. If a radio station gets hit with an FCC violation it could put them out of business. They take FCC rules very seriously. Which is to say you're going to have to be stringent about giving them content that is safe for them to play on-air. This means no curse words and certain other material that could be depend harmful or inappropriate for general public consumption.

Fun fact, comedian George Carlin used the "seven dirty words" in a 1972 monologue called "Seven Dirty Words You Can Never Say on

Television." At the time these seven words (shit, piss, fuck, cunt, cocksucker, motherfucker, and tits) were considered inappropriate and not used in scripts on television or radio. A radio broadcast using these words actually led to a Supreme Court Case that helped to define what the government had the authority to regulate in broadcast media."

There are certain words some might consider vulgar that are allowed to be spoken, but they have to be used in context – i.e. it can be left in if it is integral to the meaning of what the person is saying and is not derogatory. Example: calling someone an "ass" is not allowed, but referring to one's own "ass" could be acceptable. There is a fine line, however, and you should familiarize yourself with the FCC rules before doing this. You always have the option to bleep out a word or phrase to ensure the flow of the language isn't disrupted by cutting it completely. Inappropriate material is not limited to curse words, the FCC outlines the standards for obscene, profane, indecent, and violent material in their guidelines.

They can be found here: https://www.fcc.gov/media/radio/public-and-broadcasting

Note: Apple podcasts does require you to select "explicit" if your content contains curse words, or inappropriate themes for younger listeners.

The disclaimer to the information I'm providing is that if you are hoping to broadcast your podcast outside of the Unites States, be aware that other countries have their own regulations and guidelines for broadcast media. The FCC only governs the U.S. Should you go through the process of pitching and being accepted by a radio station, they will provide you with their moral standards as well as what rules they strictly adhere to from the FCC guide.

Even if you are not planning to solicit radio stations to broadcast your show, it's a good idea to familiarize yourself with the guidelines. They give interesting insight into how to define *"general public consumption"* of material.

On a similar note, because podcasts aren't regulated the legal implications of certain things as it related to your material can be a bit muddled. Creative Commons worked with experts at Vogele & Associates, Stanford Center for Internet and Society, and The Berkman Center (Harvard Law) to create a free legal guide which lives on a wiki page. It is meant to act as a roadmap to help navigate some of the potential legal pitfalls of podcasting. It covers things like copyright law, publicity rights, trademark law, and other topics to consider. This quite comprehensive guide can be found here:

https://wiki.creativecommons.org/wiki/Podcasting_Legal_Guide

8. Marketing Strategy

Grow Your Audience and Build Listener Loyalty

Now that you have your digital footprint covered and you've launched your podcast it automatically goes viral right? Well, maybe, and if you do that's great for you! More than likely though, you'll need to grow your audience and gain some loyal listeners. In a world where we're all constantly watching our own stats on social media through likes, loves, re-tweets, and shares it might seem like an easy thing to do. Post your podcast, watch the engagement stats go up and up. Unfortunately, it's not that easy. Growing and gaining is a patience game. There is plenty you can do to move it along, just know that you have to be dedicated and consistent.

Quality is an extremely important factor in growing and maintaining your audience. If you're just starting out and working through getting the sound and production sounding solid, that's ok. Just make sure you're always working to improve the quality of what you are putting out into the world. I've said it before, and I'll say it again, no one is going to listen to poorly recorded or poorly produced tape. They just won't. Listeners have a myriad of options out there and if they have to strain to hear your message, they likely aren't going to put in the intellectual work to do so.

Another quality factor to consider is something I've talked about already as well and that is ensuring your podcast is tight in terms of content, mission, and methodology. Are you getting the best guests?

Are you asking them the right questions? Are you posting regularly and consistently? Are you sticking to your format? Listeners will tune out if your podcast is inconsistent and unreliable.

Really consider your audience. Use the stats given to you in your hosting site to your advantage, but also do your research. Don't assume your audience is just like you. Who is this podcast appealing to? Who do you want it to appeal to? Find out more about the people who fall into your target audience. Demographics, age, socio-economics, interests, lifestyle, and preferences. Once you have built a comprehensive analysis of who your audience is, appeal to them. Tweak your podcast to hit as many common denominators as possible within your target audience.

Network everywhere all the time. Attend podcasting events or events that are related to what you talk about on your podcast. Bring postcards, fliers, or business cards with you that information about your podcast. Connect with people and tell them why they should listen.

Having as much exposure as possible will also help you grow your audience. Make sure you are easily discoverable by ensuring your podcast is on all major distribution sites. Use keywords in your descriptions everywhere the podcast has a presence online to utilize SEO (search engine optimization) as much as possible. If you don't know how SEO works, do a quick Google search to familiarize yourself. The logic is relatively easy to follow, think about what words people might search to find something like your podcast. Include those keywords in your descriptions, your social media about pages and bios, and most importantly in your show notes. Because show notes are attached to each episode, you have the opportunity to gain more SEO exposure from someone searching for a specific thing you might be covering in that particular episode, rather than a more general show description. Let's use my fictional *Barriers of Art* podcast as an example. More than likely, people will not be naturally searching for something like *"barriers of art"* unless they are specifically looking for my podcast. In my descriptions (literally everywhere) I'd use keywords like:

Visitor experience, public, museum, museum experience, art, contemporary art, conversations about art, art podcast, etc.

Make complimentary content. Put out additional content into the world. It obviously, should be adjacent to your podcast in terms of topics and themes. Write a blog or make videos to share on your social media and website. Anything that can get you more visibility is a good thing. Plus, your listeners will like having the option to find out more if something in one of your episodes strikes their fancy. You can certainly build on things you've touched on in the podcast or completely rework the content into a new delivery system. For example, you could use one of those online audiogram editors to make a short video with text. Pick a particularly engaging block of audio and feed it into one of those animated text video programs to make a really cool video to share online. People LOVE those because we are 6x more likely to remember what we see versus what we've read or heard online.

Get yourself an interview. Being a guest on someone else's podcast who may have more reach than you is a great way to gain new listeners. If you've done all the work above to join groups and networks of like-minded people and podcasters you already have a plethora of options at your fingertips. Reach out to podcasters in similar genres and let them know you're open to being on their show.

Then, go on their show, be awesome, and plug your podcast. It's also fun to be in the guest's shoes for once!

Lastly, **get reviews!** Don't be afraid to ask your network, your current listeners, your friends, family, your family's friends, and anyone who will listen to leave you a review. Star reviews are great, but written reviews are even better! Let people know it would help you enormously if they left a review. All they can say is "*no*." You've got nothing to lose.

Connecting with Your Audience

Using Online Communities to Your Advantage

Hopefully you started building your community around your podcast prior to launching, but it is imperative to keep that going. Thanks to the internet it is so easy to connect with your audience. You can do this through your personal or professional networks, social media, or even on your webpage. In this ever-changing fast-paced world people crave finding a community that they can connect with, so give them that through your podcast. Make a social network group on Facebook where fans can share their own experiences. Raising your listeners up with call outs and support will keep them engaged and make them spread the word about your podcast even further.

Use your website. Host extra content or share interesting things your fans send you. Create a contact form so people can reach out to you personally. Obviously, make a special email for your podcast so you are not giving out personal information. Additionally, make a form on your website where people can submit questions! You don't have to add a segment to your podcast where you answer listener questions. You can host a special day on the internet. As in, every Wednesday you answer a listener question on Facebook and twitter. Make it an event or just answer at your leisure through the social media channels.

Tag your guests anywhere and everywhere. When you have guests on your show, don't forget to tag them! Your listeners will appreciate learning more about them. The guest will then have the opportunity to re-share your posting with your info and that will help you get more new listeners as well as help your current listeners feel more connected to your content.

Using Marketing to Connect with Your Audience

As far as more traditional marketing goes. Social media ads are a great way to reach your targeted audience. You can select who you want to have your ads shown to in terms of demographics, age, location, lifestyle etc. helping you get new listeners and market to the ones you already have. It is *always* best to start here.

Purchasing targeted ads is also beneficial because it helps you reach who is most likely to listen to your show for the least amount of money. Focus your marketing on who it's going to work on first and then once you have a great listener base and solid stats you can start to think about other audiences to target and attract. The different types of social media platforms that you can advertise on are:

Social Networking: Facebook and LinkedIn

Microblogging: Twitter and Tumbler

Photo Sharing: Instagram, Snapchat, Pinterest

Video Sharing: YouTube, Facebook Live, Vimeo

According to bigcommerce.com[5] the best places to spend your ad money right now are: Facebook, Instagram, Twitter, Pinterest, LinkedIn, and Snapchat.

If you're not a marketing wizard and the idea of creating a bunch of ads for social media feels impossible to you, do not fear. You already have everything you need.

- Always use an image, video, or animated text video.

- Pull your texts from your description or taglines, or even actual content from your podcast.

- Make user generated content into ads. This works particularly well for small businesses who are selling a product, but it can also be applied to your podcast! For a company or small business that is selling an item or service it would look like a slideshow of sorts of people's posts about the product. Like an image of them on Instagram wearing the sweater the bought, with their caption reviewing it over the image.

- Create a similar effect by taking screen shots of Apple Podcast reviews, or posts fans have made delivering a testimonial about how great it is. Just make sure you ask give them credit and ask first if you are taking something off a listener's social media.

---

[5] https://www.bigcommerce.com/blog/social-media-advertising/#the-6-best-social-networks-for-ecommerce-advertising

If you want your ad to be a graphic design, use the free program I mentioned before – Canva. They have tons of templates and ideas formatted specifically for social media.

Hashtags

Utilizing hashtags is another great way to make yourself more discoverable and to gain some free marketing by getting your podcast in front of people. Come up with a few options. You'll want to have one that is specifically the name of your show, but also one that is catchier and along the lines of a tagline (in a few words though, rather than an entire sentence). Also include hashtags that are super obvious and will help people find you. For my *Barriers of Art* podcast, I'd choose: #barriersofart #behindthescenes #thetruthofit #contemporaryart #museums #museumeducation #publicart #visualart #installationstation #painting #photography etc.

Make sure there are two main hashtags that will always be tied to your posts about your show; you can switch up the others based on the episode you are posting about. For me, those two would be: #barriersofart and #installationstation.

Calls to Action

Another proven way to connect with your listeners is through calls to action. The more likes and comments you get on a post, the more likely it is to show up in someone's feed. That's how the algorithms work. To go viral you need 100,000 likes, but the visibility sweet spot for your current followers is 100-500 likes (the range depends on how many accounts your listeners follow or how many friends they have). When you post something ask a question that a listener can't help but want to answer. Even better, make up a call to action that gets people to post their own stories and tag you. A basic call to action would look something like this:

(photo of museum visitor in front of art)

"John Doe shares with us his interpretation of Jane Small's Lying in Wait at the Art Institute of Chicago. He divulged, 'it looks like a brick house with wings that I'd be happy to fly around in." If this cozy house could fly, where would you take it?

A call to action that requires more than a comment could read like this:

(photo of the work installed in museum)

"Have you seen Jane Small's Lying in Wait and listened to Episode 13 where we dive into the true meaning behind the piece? Post a photo of yourself in front of the installation letting us know what you think...we might just interview you for our next episode! Use #imlyinginwait and tag @barriersofart so we can see your post."

The most important thing in any marketing strategy is to pay attention to what works and then be consistent with it. Since the overhead is low for digital advertising, as in free or low-paid, you have a lot of freedom to try things out. Watch the likes and comments and use the stats tracking on your host as well as through the paid social media ad backend to figure out what posts are performing at their best. Stick to that line of posting until you need a new direction. Just like your podcast, always be evolving, listening, and modifying.

Be Consistent

Be sure to post regularly. Come up with a social media posting schedule for yourself and stick to it. You can use programs like *HootSuite* and *OnPublish* to schedule posts in advance to make it easier on yourself. Spend a few hours at the beginning of the week making and scheduling posts so you don't have to remember to do it every day. According to volusion.com[6] this is how often you should be posting on each platform:

- **Facebook**: 1-2 times a day.

- **Twitter**: 5-10 times a day.

- **Pinterest**: 5-30 pins a day.

- **LinkedIn**: 20 times per month.

- **Instagram**: 1-2 times a day.

Don't post just to post, however, studies show consistent high-quality posts that actually say something are more likely to be engaged with than a bunch of random posts without real content behind them. Use your judgement, but if it seems like you can't come up with something good, or there's nothing to share in that moment, then don't share.

---

[6] https://www.volusion.com/blog/how-often-should-you-post-on-social-media/

Where Do You Look for Listener Feedback

I keep talking about using your listener feedback, analytics, and stats to help you focus your message, but where do you find those things?

It would be prudent to set up a *"Google alert"* for your name and your podcast name. You have the ability to adjust the settings so you receive an email every time someone mentions your podcast on the internet, or you can get those emails once a day, once a week etc. This won't cover things like tagging you on social media, but it will alert you to any press, blogging, or other internet posts you wouldn't be able to find without googling yourself. Making a *"Google alert"* is awesome because you only do it once and then you don't have to remember to Google your podcast every once in a while, to be informed about what's going on with it on the internet. Just search *"Google alert"* and follow the steps to create the appropriate alert. It is them linked to your google account, making it easy to go in and adjust later on if you need to.

Reviews

The first place to look for listener feedback is in the reviews. Apple podcast reviews are the cream of the crop in terms of ratings that matter. You can also find reviews on other distribution sites like Stitcher. Unfortunately, the reviews and ratings don't convalesce in one spot. Meaning you'll need to look at all of the places where your podcast is posted that has a review option to check on the status of your reviews and ratings.

Social Media and Podcast Email

Check social media for places where you or your show are tagged. Search your hashtags to find accounts that have posted about your podcast. If you are directly tagged in something, you'll obviously get an alert so be sure and check that out to see what your audience is telling you.

You also should have set up an e-mail for your podcast. Ideally this is the email that is also linked to your apple podcast account. There is the option to make that information visible in apple podcasts. If you do not want to do that then advertise this email elsewhere, like in your Instagram or twitter bio, or on your website.

Statistics

Even though it's not directly related to specific feedback, checking your stats in your hosting site can give you valuable insight into your audience. Monitor what episodes are performing well, how often they are downloaded. When you get new subscribers. Was it immediately after your 3rd episode dropped or 2 days later, or was it when a friend made a special post promoting your podcast? Use that information to determine what is working and what isn't and then put that information to use through your marketing and posting plan! You can also apply it to future content. If your 5th episode is performing considerably higher than the others, do a spin off, or reach out to your listeners to find out what they liked about that particular episode.

Soliciting Feedback

Now that you know *where* to look for listener feedback, *how* do you solicit feedback? You should have that contact form or email set up on your website encouraging people to contact you, but if it's been quiet on the front of reviews and other contact – reach out to your fans and ask them what they want to hear! You should already be tailoring your episodes to your target audience, but now that you have a bit of a listener base it's always a good idea to throw a net into the world and see what you catch. Your audience may have things they'd love for you to cover, or people they want you to interview. Encourage them to reach out. Do this through social media and email blasts, but also do this by adding it to your outro on a few episodes. Record something like this:

I always appreciate thoughts, comments, and feedback. If you liked what you heard, or even if you didn't, reach out to me on twitter or shoot me an email via the contact sheet on my website www [dot] barriers of art [dot] com. You just might have the next great idea for an episode and if you do, I want to hear about it and anything else on your mind!"

9. How to Monetize a Podcast

Not everyone wants to find ways to monetize a podcast. You could be in it for the community, the relationship-building, or just the satisfaction of making something that's entirely yours and can help other people. If you do want to cover the overhead of your podcast or are looking to make a little money from it there are some options. Bear in mind it will take time and some work to get there, but it is feasible.

Start by making a budget for your podcast. I know, adulting. Having a clear budget will help you take stock of what is reasonable when it comes to the fees associated with podcasting. It will also help you figure out what costs you need to cover and how much money you need to go from red to black and further to profit. Include things like: recording equipment, cloud storage or hard drives, audio editing software, hosting, remote recording apps, producer, website hosting, marketing, music licensing, and your time. Break it down by start-up costs and ongoing expenses. For example, recording equipment and music licensing may be one-time purchases, whereas hosting and cloud storage are monthly (ongoing) expenses. If you want to get really professional include what you are getting for free now. Your time, for example, or if you have a producer friend who is going to partner with you to produce your podcast so you don't have to pay anyone. List those as *"in-kind"* items. Having things like that built into your budget gives you a very clear birds eye view of your whole project. That way, when you get your podcast off the ground and are ready to grow by paying yourself or others, you'll already have the framework built in.

Here is a basic example to explain how one show might determine its costs. The cost of the show varies depending on the type of podcast and level of professionalism when it comes to hiring professional to support you.

EQUIPMENT OR ONE-TIME COSTS	AMOUNT	UNIT	COST	TOTAL
EDITING SOFTWARE	1	Year	$300	$300
DIGITAL RECORDER	2	Flat	$250	$250
MICROPHONE(S)	2	Flat	$300	$300
XLR CABLES	2	Flat	$15	$30
DIGITAL STORAGE	2	Flat	$100	$200
ORIGINAL MUSIC	1	Flat	$300	$300
Total EQUIPMENT				**$1,380**

PRODUCTION	AMOUNT	UNIT	COST	TOTAL
RESEARCH & BOOKING	1	Flat	$50	$50
PRODUCTION STAFF: EXEC PRODUCER	1	Flat	$1000	$700
PRODUCTION STAFF: HOST	1	Flat	$900	$600
PRODUCTION STAFF: ASSOCIATE PRODUCER	1	Flat	$700	$400
PRODUCTION STAFF: SOUND ENGINEER	1	Flat	$300	$300
STUDIO RENTAL	2	Hours	$100	$200
TRANSCRIPTION	3	Hours	$20	$60
RSS FEED/HOSTING SERVICE	1	Month	$15	$15
SOUND FX/ MUSIC LIBRARY	1	Month	$15	$15
Total PRODUCTION				**$2,340**

PROMOTION/MARKETING	AMOUNT	UNIT	COST	TOTAL
WEBSITE	1	Month	$20	$20
EPISODE ART	1	Flat	$75	$75
SOCIAL MEDIA	1	Flat	$30	$30
POSTCARDS	100	One-Time	$0.50	$50
BUTTONS	100	One-Time	$0.25	$25
HATS	100	One-Time	$5	$500
TOTE BAGS	100	One-Time	$4	$300
Total PROMOTION				**$1,000**

Advertising and Sponsorships

Direct Advertising

Most big advertisers aren't going to consider advertising with a podcast until it hits 100,000 downloads. Don't let that deter you though, there are other advertising options out there. You can reach out to small businesses that are directly related to your podcast.

Because podcasts are so intimate and specific, people tend to buy the things you are advertising because they trust you. Even if you are small and just starting out you have something to offer, use that knowledge to your advantage when shopping for advertisers.

Podcasts ads are calculated based on something called CPM, which stands for Cost per Mile. In this case a mile is one thousand listens, therefore, that translates to cost per thousand listens.

There are three places an ad typically goes in a podcast:

Pre-roll: Ads at beginning.

Mid-roll: Ads in the middle.

Post-Roll: Ads at the end.

Pre- and mid-rolls are always the most valuable because they are pretty much guaranteed to be heard, not everyone listens to the outro, end credits, and last ad of a podcast. More often than not, they just turn it off once you sign off, or if they let it play until the end they are typically tuned out and not listening closely to an ad.

What does that look like in terms of figuring out how much to charge? If you are offering a 15 second pre-roll and a 60 second mid-roll at a rate of $25 per thousand listens and you get an average of 20,000 listens per episode, you'd charge your advertiser $500 per episode. More listeners equate more money.

Some hosting sites make it really easy for you to connect with advertisers. The hosts I already talked about in Chapter 7 offer a monetization option. Generally, what that means, is the host partners with advertisers who are specifically looking to run ads on relevant podcasts. Marketing specialists are no dummies, they know podcasts are the present and future for consumed media. If you turn that monetization option on in your host, you'll be paired with potential advertisers who will likely just provide you with a script. You'd then read that spot and produce it into your episode. Sometimes, they will provide you with an actual commercial, but that is atypical. Advertisers are choosing to showcase their product or service with you because they know your listeners trust you. If it sounds like you are just recommending a product, rather than running a previously produced ad, your listeners are more likely to purchase the goods and services you are speaking about. On that note, your listeners feel a personal bond with you, they know you and they listen because they trust you. Don't promote or advertise a product or service you can't get behind. Money is appealing, but do your research and ensure you are comfortable selling whatever the thing is.

Sponsorships

A traditional sponsorship follows the same protocol for figuring out the price via the above CPM method. Typically, you'd enter into more of a package deal with a sponsor than a few random ads with advertisers looking to buy per episode. A sponsor is more of a long-term option as they want more exposure. This is a case where your sponsor is going to need to be in line with the theme of your podcast. For example, if your podcast is about craft beer, you'd likely look for a sponsor that is a brewery or beer distributor. Sponsors will do a large ad buy ensuring that they are the only (or close to) the only ad you are running on your podcast. Think $1,000 for 4 episodes or more for the whole season. You'll just have to negotiate using the math above for how many listens and downloads you have and what makes sense for both of your budgets.

In addition to your hosting site, or if your host doesn't offer assistance with monetization, there are companies out there that will connect you with advertisers. Sometimes they will broker deals for you and take a commission, it just depends on their set-up. Here are a few to look into:

Advertisecast: www.advertisecast.com

True Native Media: www.truenativemedia.com

Adopter Media: www.adopter.media

Midroll: www.midroll.com

Affiliate Relationships

If you are familiar with social media influencers, you more than likely already know what an affiliate relationship is. These don't necessarily result in cold hard cash, but they do have monetary benefits for you. Essentially what you are doing is sharing a link and some sort of sign-up promotional code with your listeners for a product, service, or app. Something along the lines of, *"Sign up for Audible using audible.com/joinjohnspodcast and you'll receive a free subscription for 30 days!"* Affiliate relationships work more like a trade. In this case, your listener gets something out of using your link, like a discount on goods or services, but you would get either a small amount of money per sign-up or money added to your Audible account.

Unlike sponsorships, these affiliate relationships don't necessarily need to have anything to do with your podcast topic. They are more along the lines of general life things that you yourself would actually use in your normal life. Services like cell phone plans, Airbnb or other travel sites, and subscription services are just some examples.

One of the benefits to starting with an affiliate relationship is that you can do this immediately and don't need a ton of listeners to be considered. Since these companies are not paying you a marketing budget or are offering you a trade, there isn't much risk of loss for them. These can also be great ways to get some of your general life expenses covered, which in the grand scheme of things supports your podcast. The other great thing about this option is that the links are an ongoing live link. Meaning, they potentially can earn you benefits for months and even years.

The downside, of course, is that it's not income you have a way of tracking with any certainty. Because it is reliant on listeners using the link and following through with signing up for the goods or services you don't have a way to anticipate how much you will make back. It's not nothing, however, when you're just starting out everything helps!

Listener Support

Asking for money is daunting for most people. It shouldn't be though; you have people who want to support your dream of launching and maintaining a podcast. If you are really passionate about this project, it won't be hard to sell people on the idea. Crowdfunding is a great option for podcasts that are just starting out or have some sort of specific expense required of them i.e. a road trip to interview people, or a visit to a research center in another country.

Set up a Kickstarter campaign or Indiegogo to get the help you need to get your podcast off the ground. There are plenty of tutorials on the internet to help you launch a successful crowdfunding campaign.

For ongoing support, you can set up a Patreon account or link a PayPal account to your podcast website. If you are doing this just be sure to make people aware that they can donate any time to help keep your podcast going. Do that by including a message in your general podcast outro directing people to where they can donate. Include the messaging in every e-mail blast and on any printed marketing you might make to promote your podcast.

Merchandise and Live Events

Perhaps the most fun way to get some costs covered is through creative merchandise and live events. You should definitely have merchandise. It's often inexpensive and purchased in bulk, once you mark it up a bit (retail mark-up is traditionally 20-50%) you'll make your money back in sales. Be creative with your offerings though, don't just put your podcast logo on a t-shirt. For example, if I was going to make merch for my *Barriers of Art* podcast, I'd probably look into a paint by number kit, or print a funny quote about art on a t-shirt or painting apron. Maybe I'd get some painter's pallets made with the name of the show on it.

Hosting a live event like a party or live podcast episode is also a great way to make money if you can partner with a venue. You could ask that the venue donate 15% of the bar money to you and sell tickets to the event. If you have a podcast about cooking you could host a private pop-up dinner party at a chef friend's house and charge people money to attend. Be creative and craft the event around your podcast niche.

Other Options

Another more creative option is to sell your own content. One way to do this is to keep your newer episodes free, but charge for archived material. You can charge a small amount, around $2 per episode for past seasons or the past month's worth of episodes. I wouldn't recommend going this route until you have a substantial following as you don't want to deter newcomers from listening to your show.

You can also re-purpose your content into a service like books, e-books, or courses. This is particularly effective if your show is educational or motivational. For example, if your podcast is about helping your target audience combat burn out, you could write a book or lead an online workshop that goes deeper into teaching people how to prevent or recover from some specific type of burn out.

CONCLUSION

lways be making something, don't let yourself get bored. Challenge yourself to keep listening, give yourself critical feedback, take what people say to heart and always work towards being better. If it ever feels like too much, circle back to your lynch pin, the real heart of why you are doing this – your passion. Passion will always lead the way. Don't lose sight of your mission statement!

No one really knows what podcasting is going to look like in 10 years, 20 years, or heck, even 2 years from now. As a long-standing professional in broadcast media, I can confidently say podcasting is the future. It's not going anywhere and will only grow in importance. Podcasts will reach and build communities we couldn't even dream of before. If you have something to say, say it. Use what you've learned here to make something you are proud of and shout it from the roof tops. Happy podcasting!

Appendix I

Audio & Photo Consent and Release Form

Without expectation of compensation or other remuneration, now or in the future, I hereby give my consent to [legal entity/organization], its affiliates and agents, to use my voice and/or any interview statements from me in its publications, advertising or other media activities (including the Internet). This consent includes, but is not limited to:

(a) Permission to interview, film, photograph, tape, or otherwise make a video reproduction of me and/or record my voice;

(b) Permission to use my name; and

(c) Permission to use quotes from the interview(s) (or excerpts of such quotes), the film, photograph(s), tape(s) or reproduction(s) of me, and/or recording of my voice, in part or in whole, in its publications, in newspapers, magazines and other print media, on television, radio and electronic media (including the Internet), in theatrical media and/or in mailings for educational and awareness.

This consent is given in perpetuity, and does not require prior approval by me.

Name: _____

Signature:_____

Address: _____

_____

Date: _____

The below signed parent or legal guardian of the above-named minor child hereby consents to and gives permission to the above on behalf of such minor child.

Signature of Parent
or Legal Guardian: _____ Print Name: _____

The following is required if the consent form has to be read to the parent/legal guardian:
I certify that I have read this consent form in full to the parent/legal guardian whose signature appears above.

_____   _____
Date   Signature of Organizational Representative or Community Leader

Your Opinion

First of all, thank you for purchasing this book. I know you could have picked any number of books to read, but you picked this book and for that I am extremely grateful.

If you enjoyed this book and found some benefit in reading this, I'd like to hear from you and hope that you could take some time to post a review on Amazon.

I wish you all the best for your podcasting journey!

About the Author

Amanda Roscoe Mayo is a curator of contemporary culture, podcast producer, radio station director, and music enthusiast. She got her start in radio with NPR station Marfa Public Radio in very far West Texas. In that vast and beautiful desert, she caught the interviewing bug and has ridden the wave into podcasting. From 2012-2014 she was a contributing music, art, and  film writer for KQED Arts – the online publication for San Francisco NPR station KQED. Additionally, she was a music journalist for Consequence of Sound and other publications. Since 2014 she has been a dual Production and Features Director at Chicago Independent Radio Project (CHIRP) in Chicago, where she manages an award-winning weekly artist interview podcast. Amanda is the founder of, How to Podcast, a podcasting coaching business where she uses her industry expertise to guide clients through the process of developing and implementing a podcast from the ground up.

Made in the USA
Monee, IL
22 December 2022

23337142R10081